Praise for *I Love You, Son*

"Rick Meyer walks the road of male experience with empathy, vulnerability, and compassion—and gives us an opportunity to join the pilgrimage. This reflective book blends personal experience, spiritual discernment, and good developmental theory into an almost devotional style, ripe for deep reflection and conversation."

> —*Bruce M. Hartung, Ph.D., associate professor of practical theology, Concordia Seminary, Saint Louis*

"Rick Meyer touches upon the core issues with which men struggle. His keen insight as a pastoral counselor brings to life men's anxiety with intimacy, vulnerability, and self-insight, and connects these concerns with the core message of the Gospel of Jesus Christ. This is a book for the head and the heart."

> —*Rev. Paul G. Hill, director, Center for Youth Ministries of Wartburg Seminary*

"*I Love You, Son* will give counselors, pastors, professional and lay men's leaders, and youth and family ministers a deeper understanding of the wounds men carry, and what the church can do to provide healing so that men can be made whole participants in building family, congregation, and community."

> —*Doug Haugen, director, Lutheran Men in Ministry*

I Love You, Son

What Every Boy (and Man) Needs to Hear

Rick Meyer

Augsburg Books
MINNEAPOLIS

To My Parents, Whom I Love

Table
of
Contents

Introduction

Why I Wrote This Book

In this book about fathers and sons, I contend that every child should know he is deeply loved and cherished and that when a child does not have this assurance, persistent emotional deficits often follow. I further contend that males experience and express these deficits in unique ways in our society. *I Love You, Son* is a compilation of case studies that reflect the struggles of adolescent boys and adult males as they face their own emotional deficits in relation to God, self, and others.

The boys and men whose stories I share in these pages have graciously allowed me to journey with them through some of the most difficult and challenging times of their lives. The stories are powerful and compelling, and cannot be read casually. Because of the tenderness and vulnerability of the boys and men in these stories, it is hoped that the reader will be drawn to participate in the quest for what it means to be a man in our world today. As a result of sharing these stories, I want fathers to go home and wrestle with their sons (see Luke, age 9), to hug and hold their stepsons (Kevin, age 14), and to help their sons learn a wider range of emotional expression than just anger and withdrawal (Aaron, age 16). I want men to hear the voice of God's forgiveness in the face of infidelity (Mark, age 40), to learn that both closeness and distance are necessary for true intimacy to occur (Adam, age 34), to discover that, with help, sexual addictions can be overcome (Sam, age 43), and to find that midlife can signal new opportunities for renewal in our most important relationships (Robert, age 59).

This writing grows out of my own experience as a son and as a father; it emerges also from my experience as an ordained pastor and as a professional counselor who works with boys and men. I have often been frustrated by the limited number of good books available in the area of men's studies. I frequently notice that books written by men are overly focused on the writer's ability and expertise as a professional and insufficiently focused on his own personal feelings of vulnerability. In other words, the material is too polished. The authors don't seem to make many mistakes or demonstrate much self-doubt. They appear nearly untouchable, unapproachable—especially those authors who propose a "solution focused" 3-step, 7-step, or 10-step program for success. Maybe this stuff sells, but it sounds more like Wall Street and Disneyland than real life. Real life, as I understand it, is messy. It consists of beauty and ambivalence, hopefulness and fear, delight and pain, and all-too-rarely a feeling of competency when it comes to participating in a family as a husband and father. The stories in this book, and the lessons that can be discerned from them, address this messiness without fear of vulnerability and with no illusion of easy step-by-step instructions for improvement.

My desire in writing this book is to contribute to the conversation about what it means to be male in our society today and to encourage and challenge men in their efforts as husbands and fathers (especially as fathers). I want to extend the voice of God, who spoke from heaven with pride in his son, Jesus, saying, "This is my son, whom I love" (Matthew 3:17). The desire of my heart is that every boy and man feel deeply cherished by both our heavenly father and an earthly father.

How I Wrote This Book

I think it's important that the reader know something about how I approached the writing of this book. What I hope becomes clear is that I am as much a participant in the struggles depicted here as I am an observer. In fact, this movement between participation and observation is the same process to which I invite the reader. We must enter life fully and also learn from it. And this process is both painful and joyous at the same time.

I notice a four-way dialogue going on whenever I talk with men in a therapeutic setting. The first conversation is between me and the man who is sitting in front of me. The second conversation is my internal discussion with myself about my own experiences. The third conversation is between me and the other authors I have read. And the fourth conversation is between me and God. This fourth conversation, I have discovered, is especially important as I trust that God can see beyond my experience, and as such can help me suspend judgment toward another person (including myself) until I gain a fuller view of that person's experiences and perspective.

My belief system is an inseparable part of who I am as a person, and consequently it finds expression in my roles as husband, father, pastor, and counselor. I'm not always clear about my beliefs and assumptions, but I have discovered the importance of continuing to work at clarifying these for myself. Because all of us are in process, we can never fully know another person or ourselves. I believe that because God is at work in our lives and leads us to see ourselves more clearly, we need to always be open to surprises. For this reason I believe that every encounter I have with another person is not by mere chance. Rather, God has guided such an encounter for my benefit and that of the other, even if (perhaps especially so) a particular encounter is difficult and painful. Proverbs 27:17 says it this way, "As iron sharpens iron, so one man sharpens another."

Although I take great comfort in a number of references to scripture, I also struggle to apply much of what I read. In other words, I approach my understanding and application of scripture with humility. I don't suggest that one can find a scripture passage for every situation in life—a kind of religious 3-step prescription process. Far from it. I am more likely to feel affinity with the passage that tells us, "Work out your salvation with fear and trembling" (Philippians 2:12). However, every belief system, and we each have one, has its road marks.

My belief system includes the idea that God enjoys a place of both imminence (a presence here with us in time and space) and transcendence (a place above and beyond time and space). Such transcendence helps me to accept what St. Paul says in his first letter to the church in Corinth: "Now [on this side of heaven] I know in part; then [on the other side of heaven] I shall know fully" (1 Corinthians 13:12). Paul was humble enough to recognize that his view of life, of God, and of others, and perhaps especially of himself, was limited, even fragmentary. He believed in ultimate truth and reality, but also realized that only God can see fully.

I believe that God originally created everything to not have any tendencies toward destructiveness. However, through the rebellion of human beings, the nature of all creation changed to now include such horrors as affliction, sickness, and death. It was because of God's unfailing love for his creation that he sought to rescue us from our fallen state by giving us the assurance of his forgiveness through the death and resurrection of his son, Jesus. And though the messiness of life still remains on this side of heaven, all will be reversed—back to God's originally intended will for his creation—when Jesus returns in glory.

Within my faith life I carry the understanding that God is with me, and that by his Spirit he leads, guides, shapes, and transforms my thoughts, emotions, and behaviors. I view my fallen state and my brokenness as a stubborn closed fist that pushes against the open hand of the Spirit that covers it. The hand of the Spirit is stronger, but never without resistance. As I work with boys and men, I seek to help them listen to the voice of God's Spirit that embraces their stubbornness and leads them to see that only in our weakness do we feel God's true strength. It's not until we reach a vulnerable state that we can hear the voice from heaven that says, "This is my son, whom I love."

The Boys I See

Introduction to Adolescent Males

During the past few years, I have seen my counseling work with adolescents increase dramatically. I love to work with these kids, both boys and girls, in part because I find them so enlivened by the slightest bit of affirming adult attention. But it seems especially true that most of them are lacking the presence of a significant adult male in their lives. Whether the distance has been created by divorce or by neglect or some other form of abuse, these kids are often expected to function in the face of serious emotional deficits.

My heart goes out to these kids. I want to help fill the emotional void. And I hope, especially with the boys, to provide a safe place for them to learn a language for emotions, so that they will have a wide range of expression—something other than aggression and withdrawal.

I often think that the labels we place on children—depression, behavior disorders, ADHD—can be translated, in part, into "lack of hugs," "absence of positive regard," and "no clear adult leadership." How interesting it is to observe that when a couple begins to address marital conflicts more effectively, their "troubled" teen becomes more cooperative and a pleasure to be around. Could it be that a child's acting-out behavior is often just a symptom of a larger family problem?

One

The Abandoned Child

David, age 15

David is a bright, intelligent boy who has a difficult time mainstreaming and is always in trouble. When he puts forth a modicum of effort, he gets A's and B's. However, he is easily distractable, and if he is not careful, he can slip to C's and D's. ADHD, behavior disorders, depression, poor impulse control—there is no lack of labels available for this kid. He fit them all at one time or another. What brought him to counseling, though, was a recent suicidal ideation. He had told his school counselor that he wanted to die.

From an early age David has been bounced back and forth between his divorced biological parents. He lived with his mother first, until she felt unable to deal with him. Besides, her new husband physically abused David, so she decided he should live with his dad. David's mother told him he was just going for a visit, but she never returned to pick him up from his father's house. His father worked about eighty hours a week, partied often, and had different women stay overnight. David was confused, hurt, isolated, and growing increasingly violent toward classmates. "I hit kids first, then ask questions later," he told me. "I'm not afraid of anyone."

The truth is, David was always afraid. He never had the opportunity to feel the security that comes with a consistent home environment. At the time of our visits, the most stable adult/parent figure in David's life was his father's live-in girl-friend. Fortunately she had a tender place in her heart for this boy. In fact, she was the one who insisted on counseling and paid for it out of her own pocket. Sometimes God's gifts come from the most surprising sources.

David and I met weekly for several months. He loved to come for counseling. As with so many of the kids I see, he looked forward to our visits and expressed disappointment when he couldn't come. Parents often warn me that their child probably won't be very talkative or cooperative. I usually experience just the opposite. I have a hard time getting a word in edgewise. And these kids don't just remain on the surface. They dig deep and talk about what's really on their minds. I love working with these kids, which is probably why they open up to me.

Another reason I enjoy working with adolescents is that it gives me an opportunity to remember some of my own life-shaping adolescent experiences. I believe that I could have been greatly helped by an adult taking a genuine interest in me. I want these kids to feel cherished, important, special, beloved of God. I want them to have hope for the future. I want them to have what I didn't have, namely, self-respect. How can they be asked to love others when they don't love themselves? "Love your neighbor *as* yourself" (Luke 10:27, emphasis added) were Jesus' words on the subject. Has anyone ever modeled the love of God toward these kids? I wish all parents could see that their most important job is building their relationship with their children.

Early in my meetings with David, I had identified him as an "edge kid." This is a term I coined to describe kids who have one foot over the line, or "edge," toward isolation and withdrawal from their family. I saw David as someone who was susceptible to hooking up with the wrong crowd and experimenting with alcohol and other drugs. My observations were confirmed when he confided in me that he and a friend had recently tried sniffing air-conditioning coolant. He said, "That's the best I've ever felt." And that's exactly what I was afraid of. Would he do it again? How far would he go next time? Could I help him learn to feel good enough about himself that he wouldn't continue down this self-medicated path? How do I make a change in this boy without also effecting a change in his primary emotional system, namely, his family?

One day David brought a CD into our counseling session to play his favorite song for me. The CD was by a rocker named Kid Rock. Some of the songs on the CD were, according to the parental advisory on the cover, extremely offensive. The song David wanted to play for me, however, was called "Only God Knows Why." It was a reflective piece, and it contained a spiritual message that had great meaning for David. Although the song had plenty of rough edges and contained profanity, I learned a great deal from the words and how David applied them to his life. I could see that David was looking for positive outcomes in his life, in spite of the feeling of having been abandoned by his mother. I could sense that he did not want to become like his father, whom he described as a "miserable" person who drinks too much and is "unhappy with life." I learned that David's tendency to get in trouble at school is a conscious effort to get laughs and attention. Like the singer, he wants everybody to know his name.

It was abundantly clear that David's primary desire is to be loved. He wants to live despite hardship and adversity, as evidenced by the singer's promise that he will still be there when the listener's wall tumbles down. I learned how much David struggles with his past and misses his mother while he works to make sense of his place in the world. The song comes to an end with the assertion that, as the title indicates, "only God knows why," and closes with the image of a river, which, for David, symbolizes a baptism, a washing, a freeing, a cleansing—in short, a new beginning.

I'm glad that I took the time to listen carefully to what David heard in this song. My initial response had been to resist the song. I'm supposed to be David's counselor, not his friend. But kids often tell us about themselves through the story of someone else. David wanted me to hear him. And the song fit. The song was messy, ugly, offensive—much like David's life. He was struggling to make sense of it all. He was turning to God (and to me) for help. Do I represent God to this child? God took on human flesh in the person of his son, Jesus. This is the power of the incarnation, that God would place himself in our midst—even though our lives are often messy, ugly, offensive—to give us hope.

There are times during my counseling sessions when, like Moses before the burning bush, I want to take off my shoes because I sense that I am standing on holy ground. I can feel God breaking into the counseling relationship, perhaps in a turning point, an expression of repentance, a gleam of hope in a child's eye. Somehow all of the time and effort have been worth it. The many hours spent together in counseling have built a relationship, a safe place, a redemptive moment. In an instant my calling is confirmed. In spite of all my ignorance, awkwardness, and personal self-doubt, God has used me, and my spirit is renewed. At such a moment I could die a happy man.

David and I were developing a deep level of trust. He began to show me his writing. He had written forty-two pages of a fictitious story in which he was the central character. The first installment was just one of several chapters David intended to write. It was not a school assignment or part of an extracurricular program. He simply enjoyed writing on his own. And it was amazing. He had plot structure and character development. He had made notes in the margins for future improvements to the story. He became energized as he talked about the process of writing (and the next day he got kicked out of class for not participating).

We must find a way to tap into every child's area of interest. If David could find an avenue of expression for his passions, who knows what he could do with his talent? He seemed genuinely surprised to learn that I thought he had a special gift. "I've never shown this writing to anyone before. I was always too afraid that they would think I was stupid or weird." He went on, "Do you really think I could do something with my writing?" I had never seen so much hopefulness in him before—it consumed his entire body: the way he spoke, carried himself, expressed curiosity and playfulness. I pray we can find a creative outlet for his interests—time is definitely of the essence.

David is a boy who has never known stability and security at home, and at the age of fifteen has been on his own for about half of his life. Abandonment and fear are the only sure things that David has known in his life. It really shouldn't surprise anyone that he has difficulty respecting authority when all of his primary authority figures have failed him.

David has been conditioned to believe that others only intend him harm. Consequently, he protects himself by seeking to get the upper hand before anyone has the chance to mistreat him. Gradually, he is edging his way out of the family system and beginning to look for emotional and psychic relief in the wrong places.

I believe David has a gift for writing and creative expression that could be of benefit to others. I just hope that we can keep him alive and well long enough for him to see this giftedness in himself. David is becoming aware that God might be directing his life—but he just barely believes it.

Two

A Limited Range of Emotional Expression

Aaron, age 16

Aaron was referred to me by his school psychologist. She was concerned that Aaron was not dealing appropriately with grief. He had been flaring up at teachers and coaches, and there were recent reports of him getting caught off campus with alcohol. All of this was uncharacteristic behavior for Aaron. The incident that seemed to prompt these new behaviors happened two months prior to Aaron being referred to me: he had hit and killed an elderly woman in an automobile accident.

Aaron's parents wanted to speak with me at length before my first session with their son. They both strongly questioned the assessment of the school psychologist, saying they believed she was overreacting to normal adolescent behavior. The only reason they were bringing Aaron in was to fulfill a requirement for continued admission at his private school. "Honestly," they said, "we don't think he needs to be here, and we really don't want him here, but we'll let you talk to him and see what you think."

Great, I thought, I have a resistant kid to deal with, but even worse, resistant parents. This should go well.

When Aaron walked in he was dressed in preppy clothing, expensive shoes and jewelry, and carried himself with a defensive air that belied the fact that he had been well prepared to convince me he didn't need my help. He was a good-looking young man with intelligent eyes. I wondered how in the world, under these circumstances, I was going to connect with this kid. So I started with the truth as we both understood it. I said: "You don't want to be here. Your parents don't want you to be here. And I've never met you before so I really don't know if you need to be here or not. But the school psychologist wants a second opinion, so that's why I'm here. I suggest we make the best of it, and who knows, we might even learn something in the process. Let's see if we can keep you in school." Aaron said, "Sure, whatever." We were really cooking now.

We discussed the accident. Or rather, I discussed the accident. Aaron was bound and determined not to participate, as if he were upholding a sacred pledge. In an attempt to help Aaron access his deeper emotions, I asked him to write a letter to the woman who had died.

Dear Patricia,

I never once would have hit you on purpose. I wouldn't hit even my enemies. I shouldn't have been speeding, but we both contributed. God chose for this to happen for both of us, and I think it taught me the greatest lesson ever. We can talk about this accident when I get to heaven.

Aaron

I had requested that Aaron write a page to the woman. Instead he wrote five sentences. And though he might believe the ideas he expressed about shared responsibility and God's timing, Aaron had not found a way to access the deeper emotions associated with this tragedy. When I made this observation, he didn't understand what I was talking about. "It just happened," he said. "It's unfortunate, but it happened. That's it." I decided to talk with his parents.

As I discussed Aaron's letter with his parents, they appeared equally devoid of emotion. When I described their son as merely objective, philosophical, and self-focused about the event, his father responded, "You've just described 90 percent of the people I work with every day." He was an executive of a large company. "Bad stuff happens all the time," he continued. "You can't change it, so why dwell on it? I think my son is sorry for what happened. Now it's time to move on."

The family seemed too cold and unfeeling to imagine that they were real. I felt there must be some explanation for their suppression. I asked about whether or not charges were being brought against the family for the accident. And this helped shed some light. Their attorney had told them not to discuss the case with anyone. Unfortunately, as so often happens when attorneys become involved, the suppression fed into the grieving process and kept the family stuck at the point of denial (and a lot of money would be spent to maintain this unemotional state). If only they could set their legal fears aside long enough to help their son. Later, after building some trust, I asked Aaron to try the letter-writing exercise again.

Dear Patricia,

I am sorry for your death. I wish it wasn't me whom God chose to take your life or contribute to it, but it was. I have to live with taking your life, and your family has to live with the loss of your life. I am sure they *are angry, because I would have been also. You are in heaven with no pain and a perfect life. I have to live here on earth with the thought of me contributing to taking someone's life. I didn't know you at all and couldn't have told anyone what you looked like even. I never meant to hurt you or your loved ones. If only I had met you previously or even your family and we could have talked about this, but I'm a stranger to your family and a punk kid. I am a kid, and God works through everyone. I believe God makes everything happen for a reason. You have taught me a lot and never said a word to me.*

Aaron

This letter was clearly more genuine. Aaron still had a long way to go, but he had begun to access some of his deeper emotions. The letter demonstrates anger, hurt, loss, a glimpse of personal responsibility ("I have to live with taking your life"), and even an outward look—possibly empathy?—at how others might be feeling. If Aaron could sustain this self-reflection, he had a real chance to move through the process of grief and personal responsibility in a healthier way. Unfortunately, Aaron never got the chance, as his parents explained away his angry outbursts and drinking as "normal" adolescent behaviors. "This doesn't have anything to do with the accident," they said, "and we're not interested in blowing this out of proportion. After all, the elderly woman pulled out in front of our son and she was moving too slow for traffic."

I never saw Aaron again. He left his private school because the school psychologist still insisted on counseling. Now it was my turn to grieve.

Our society has become adept at teaching boys to deny their tender, vulnerable emotions. In fact, this socialization process seems to be a major reason that boys and men often do not have a language for intimacy in their most important relationships. The observation that men have a limited language or range of emotional expression is corroborated by Ronald Levant, a leading researcher in the area of men's studies. After reviewing some of the most current information on the male socialization process, he concludes: "Anger is, in fact, one of the few emotions boys are encouraged to express, and as a consequence, the outlawed vulnerable emotions, such as hurt, disappointment, fear, and shame, get funneled into the anger channel" ("Toward the Reconstruction of Masculinity," in *A New Psychology of Men*, edited by Ronald F. Levant and William S. Pollack, p. 240).

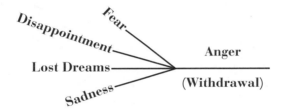

Like several streams of vulnerability (fear, disappointment, lost dreams, sadness) all flowing into one of two channels (anger, or its corollary, withdrawal), so goes the emotional system of many males. Later, in the discussion on the loop of intimacy, in chapter 12, I will describe intimacy as "the ability to share pain." And "pain" is understood to include insecurities, vulnerabilities, weaknesses, failures, dashed hopes, unrealized expectations, losses, disappointments, and fears. But more often than not, we as men don't seem to have a language for these emotions.

I'll never forget a Lamaze class my wife and I attended before the birth of our first child. The facilitator, a woman, had the couples split up into two groups, one for men and one for women. Our assignment was to list and discuss the emotions we were experiencing in anticipation of the birth of our child. The facilitator remained with the women and left us men to fend for ourselves. The outcome was predictable.

We could see that the women on the other side of the room were off and running, quickly and easily exchanging ideas. We, on the other hand, just looked at one another (and at the ground), wondering who would break the silence. Finally someone said, "I guess we better do this thing." So this same guy offered the emotion "happy." Everyone nodded with approval and made similar affirming comments. Then someone else said "excited." Again, affirming nods and comments. I decided to take a risk with the group and said "fear." The response? A couple of quiet, slow nods, and then someone said quickly "concern about money, insurance." Then silence fell over the group—an uncomfortable pause—until someone began talking about the Dallas Cowboys and other related football stories. A few minutes into this new and safe topic, one of the guys looked up at me and said, "I guess it was just a matter of time before we started talking football." We laughed and continued by talking about something other than our emotions.

When it was time for us to rejoin our wives, the facilitator asked the men to list their emotions. We had four or five to offer. The women had come up with a list of about twenty-five. I remember vividly the response of one young man in our group who, looking up with all sincerity, said, "I didn't even know there were that many emotions." I think he spoke for all of us.

One of the things I like about this story is that it illustrates the power of the socialization process that conditions boys and men to avoid their emotions. I even discovered that there is a technical word to describe the condition of a man who has a limited range of emotional expression: alexithymia (literally, "without words for emotions"). What a relief! We actually have a name for this experience. Now I can just tell people that I suffer from alexithymia. Cool!

Having a limited range of emotional expression, however, is not a matter to take lightly. As in Aaron's case, it can have significant consequences. Aaron had experienced a tragic, life-changing event: he hit another car, and the accident resulted in a woman's death. New out-of-control behaviors were beginning to appear. Fortunately, the school psychologist was perceptive and made a referral for counseling. However, the attorney representing the family said, "Be quiet," and this fed into the male-socialized tendency to deny vulnerable emotions. Aaron was just becoming more self-aware when his father and mother decided he didn't need counseling. "We're busy people," they said, "and we need to put this incident behind us and move forward."

Aaron's parents convinced themselves that his uncontrolled outbursts at school and his drinking were normal adolescent behaviors. Once again, the message to a boy is that he must channel all tender, vulnerable emotions into one acceptable mode of expression, namely, anger. The only other alternative for Aaron was withdrawal—and this was achieved by his removal from counseling.

I struggle sometimes myself to share vulnerable emotions with other men. How can I help boys and men do something that our society does not easily support? Even some women perpetuate the shameful myth of so-called nonmasculine emotions by referring to a sensitive man as "a woman in a man's body." How confusing!

Three

Facing
Life
and
Death

Justin, age 17

Justin and his family came to me the way most of my clients do, as a referral from a pastor. In fact, all of the people profiled in this book are from Christian congregations. Real people with real needs. And God created and loves each one of them.

This message, that God created and loves Justin, is the primary message Justin needed to hear. He was seventeen years old and had juvenile diabetes. He took insulin three to four times a day, and he sometimes experienced blackouts. All he wanted was to be "normal," like the other kids, to eat fast food and drink sodas. "Sometimes I overdo my splurging, and I'm afraid it will result in my premature death one day." Justin lived with death every day. And this was at a time when he was supposed to be assuming his own indestructibility and immortality. There was no shelter of denial for this kid.

Justin was referred to me because he had become increasingly self-destructive. He had stolen his mother's ATM card and withdrawn between one and two thousand dollars. He had put thirty-seven hundred miles on his car in the past two months, and he was hanging around with a known drug user. His parents had recently found a stash of empty beer cans in his closet. On top of that, he had skipped twenty-two days of school in the last three months. His mother and stepfather were at their wits' end and asking for help.

Justin also lived with the knowledge that his biological father drank himself to death when Justin was just two years old. In many ways, however, Justin was fortunate. He had a stepfather who loved him and treated him as his own son. And Justin affectionately referred to his stepfather as "Dad." This fact was a great blessing in my work with this family, as I have far too often observed stepparents who never intended to embrace the concept of parenting the children from a spouse's previous marriage. Quite honestly, I have come to the conclusion that remarriage should not occur if the stepparent shows no clear intent to parent and cherish the kids. The sacrifice that the biological parent makes by remaining single is a far better option than the hardship of displaced children.

My conversations with Justin took me to a personal place of suffering. I have a daughter who was diagnosed at two months of age with cystic fibrosis, a terminal condition that initially affects the digestive system and the lungs, though it can lead to the deterioration of several vital organs. The digestive part is fairly manageable, but there is still no significant treatment for the lungs. For my child, a common cold is nothing common at all. A cough has the potential to turn into pneumonia and cause lung damage and eventual lung collapse. How could I use what I have learned with my child to help Justin begin to hope for a future? (Do I honestly have hope for my own child? Does my relationship with God include a place for distrusting God? I remember the man who asked Jesus to heal his son. He spoke for me when he said, "I do believe; help me overcome my unbelief" [Mark 9:24].)

I knew that Justin needed to see life as bigger than diabetes.

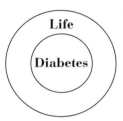

He currently had these two reversed, and diabetes was perceived as the bigger part.

Diabetes was certainly a big part of Justin's life, to be sure, but he needed to see it as smaller than life itself. And I didn't know of any other way to convey this message than by discussing the fact that God created and loved him no matter what happened. "But my dad died young. Maybe I'm supposed to die young, too." I asked him to write a letter to his biological father. In this way I hoped that Justin might be able to access his deeper emotions and begin to reflect on his father more objectively, thereby allowing him to step back and take a better look at himself and his current relationship with his family.

Dear Dad,

I'm writing this to you to tell you my feelings about your death. I am angry and sad about the way you died, and that you never took care of yourself. I don't think you understand how hurt I am that I never got to know you, and that I didn't get to grow up with you as my father. I didn't get to do anything with you, like play baseball and football, things a father and son should do together, but you left Mom to fill the void and raise me all by herself.

I really don't remember much about you, but what I do remember is all bad, and I really wish you could have been there for Mom and me instead of drinking yourself to death. The thing that hurt me the most is that you were never there for Mom and me in our time of need.

Dad, I'm going to close with saying I hope you're in a better place and are happy there. Dad, I will always love you.

Love,
Justin

Justin has had to live with great ambivalence from an early age. His father died when he was two years old, and he has had to cope with progressively deteriorating health due to juvenile diabetes. His letter is filled with hurt and hope, anger and disappointment, love and tenderness, life and death. Could Justin be attempting to get closer to his biological father through his reckless, self-destructive behaviors? His biological father killed himself with alcohol. Maybe life really isn't worth living. Maybe a better place does exist beyond this present world. Perhaps his father was the smart one after all.

Justin's life was spinning out of control. He wasn't making good judgments, and he was increasingly taking more "suicidal" risks with his life. I urged his mother and stepfather to intervene. They sent him to an in-treatment program for drug and alcohol abuse. Following this they established random drug testing and regular individual and family counseling. The family was hurting financially and had limited mental-health insurance benefits, so I made arrangements to see them for a reduced fee. How could I stop seeing Justin because he didn't have enough money for counseling? How could I convey that God both created and loved him if I wasn't willing to make a sacrifice myself? ("Lord, please help me to pay the bills so that I can continue to serve you in this way.")

I want so much for Justin to experience the beautiful and pleasurable side of life. He needs to know that when God originally created this world, he did so perfectly, without sickness and death. And God declared that the world he had created was very good. (Justin is very good). Somehow, through the rebellion of human beings, the very nature of God's creation changed; it became broken and vulnerable to illness and death. God loves his creation, the "very-good-ness" of which can still be seen and appreciated. Because of God's love for us, he will ultimately reverse all that has gone wrong when, at the end of time, our Lord returns for the resurrection—a new creation. Then Justin will know only beauty and pleasure. But for now we suffer. For now we agonize and groan. For now we feel the frequent reminders of our humble state . . . and our need for God's mercy and grace.

I sometimes wish that every parent could view life from the perspective of a parent who has a terminally ill child. Every new day takes on a precious quality. Moments are cherished—and grieved—more deeply. Deciding whether to spend more time at work or come home early is less difficult. When I first held my daughter in my arms, I thought that because of my depth of feeling, God must love her very much. As time went on, though, I discovered that God was changing me through her, and so I concluded that God must love me very much. I guess God is waiting for us to come home. He knows that our temporary sufferings will be dwarfed by eternity. I can't bear the thought of living without my child. ("Lord, I believe; help my unbelief . . . my doubt . . . my disappointment in you for allowing this to happen.")

Justin was a typical seventeen-year-old boy. He loved to drive, he loved girls, and he enjoyed taking on more responsibility while at the same time feeling sheltered from adulthood. Justin also faced his mortality every day, evidenced by injection after injection, special diets, and the deterioration of vital organs. Sometimes reality could be suspended for a short time of recklessness—a few beers with the guys—then the blackouts would wake him up again.

Anger, disbelief, even hatred—Justin needed to learn that God was big enough to take it all. He also needed permission from me, a pastor, to give full expression and voice to these feelings. This dear child needed to see God through the suffering of his son, Jesus, because a God who has experienced suffering himself seems far more believable, acceptable, and approachable.

Even Jesus cried out from the cross, "My God, my God, why have you forsaken me?" (Mark 15:34).

Because of my fears about my own child's health, I understood Justin's fears and his attempts to deny reality better than I wanted to. I can't remain in the pit of hell for very long myself before I talk my way out of it. It hurts too much. Its fires are unquenchable. It is my hope that I can help Justin understand that death is the doorway to a continuation of life, a life that begins on this side of heaven. Even more importantly, I want Justin to see that God intends to create beauty out of tragedy. And I want Justin to hear the voice of God from heaven say, "I love you, Son."

Four

An Ineffective Stepparent

Kevin, age 14

Kevin was brought to me because he and his stepfather couldn't get along. Jerry, the stepfather, had recently become so threatening that Kevin's mother took Kevin and his younger brother to a nearby motel for a few days for a cooling-off period. Kevin's unwillingness to accept his stepfather's authority had been identified by the adults as the "problem" that needed to be solved. If Kevin could just be straightened out and fixed, then all would be fine. And though Kevin's mother, Dian, was willing to come in for counseling, the stepfather initially refused, and only did so reluctantly with the stipulation that the purpose of counseling was to get *Kevin* on the right track.

When I spoke with Dian and Jerry, all I heard was how difficult Kevin had been ever since the two married. "He constantly eggs Jerry on. He can't seem to just do what Jerry tells him without a verbal fight." When I talked to Kevin alone, however, I saw a more multidimensional picture. Kevin had witnessed, from an early age, his biological father's drunkenness and verbally and physically abusive behavior toward his mother. Then Kevin endured a couple of live-in boyfriends who treated him terribly. When he eventually wanted to go and live with his biological father and his new wife and family, he was told that they didn't want him. Now, with his mother remarried, Kevin watched as Jerry and Dian shared a commitment to their biological younger son. Kevin once again felt displaced and unwanted.

Kevin was bright and articulate. His mother was an emotionally weak person, but in her clearer moments she could see the harm that she had allowed to happen to her son. Still, she became steeped in denial because she feared losing the stability of Jerry's income. In other words, when she felt afraid for Kevin, she couldn't bring herself to demand that Jerry seek help. She knew he wouldn't, and was afraid that if she pushed, he might leave altogether. As for Jerry, he had been hurt very badly as a boy himself, and was of the opinion that giving Kevin "a good pounding" would be the best thing he could do for him.

As Kevin and I spoke, it was obvious that he lived with a powerful internal conflict. On the one hand, he loved Jerry and desperately wanted to be loved back. He watched as Jerry verbalized and physically demonstrated love toward his younger brother, Jerry's biological son, but Jerry had never told Kevin that he loved him. On the other hand, Kevin was growing increasingly afraid of Jerry. Jerry even told him, "One of these days I'm gonna put you in the hospital." And Kevin believed him.

At one point I attempted to intervene on Kevin's behalf by helping his mother strengthen her shared parenting skills with Jerry. At times Jerry had tried to parent Kevin, only to have Dian undermine him in Kevin's presence, with the result being that Jerry would withdraw and shut down. I asked Dian to introduce a technique in Kevin's presence whereby the couple would carry on a conversation with Kevin about the family's issues while the two of them held hands. The conversation was going well until the focus shifted to Jerry, at which point he pulled his hand away and said, "I guess I've failed again." In the way that we can use tears to manipulate a situation, self-deprecating remarks such as this are often used to gain sympathy and thereby turn the focus away from the real issues. Jerry used this tactic often. And Dian, an incessant caretaker, generally took the bait. At their next session, the couple reported that the hand-holding exercise didn't work.

As is often the case, both parents worked full time outside the home. The younger son was in day care until 3 P.M. each day, when Kevin got home from school and took over child care duties until at least 6 P.M. The family did not financially need for both parents to work outside the home full time, but it was necessary if they were to maintain their desired lifestyle. Both parents returned from work stressed and tired and frequently unavailable emotionally. In other words, Kevin was on his own from the time he got home from school until he went to bed. He was spending excessive amounts of time in front of the television or playing computer games and was beginning to exhibit a shorter and shorter attention span. He was easily distractable and uncooperative. He seemed depressed. His grades were dropping, and he was acting out at school.

Not long after compiling this list of Kevin's symptoms, the family took a trip for spring break. They went to the country to visit grandparents. They enjoyed a much more relaxed schedule and spent time outdoors fishing and hiking. The report by the parents about this experience was nothing short of astounding. "Kevin was a different person. He demonstrated confidence and patience with family members. He and Jerry even laughed together. And Jerry put his arm around Kevin one time. Kevin beamed." But now, just two weeks back in the grind of "normal" daily living, all of the gains had been lost. Kevin and Jerry were back to their usual unhappy selves.

More than anything else I wanted Kevin to feel safe at home. I also saw an opportunity for Jerry to have a positive influence on

Kevin's life. Kevin was young enough that it wasn't too late for
Jerry to be a true father figure to him. It wouldn't have taken
much. An arm around the shoulder, a hug, an "I love you," and
Kevin would have been in Jerry's corner for the long haul.
Unfortunately, Jerry would never allow himself to become that
vulnerable with Kevin. And the harder Kevin pushed Jerry with
verbal prodding to connect emotionally, the more Jerry pushed
him away. Finally Jerry lost control. My greatest fears were realized. I received a call from Dian telling me that Jerry was in jail
and Kevin was in the hospital. Jerry had made good on his promise. He had shown Kevin what it meant to be a "real" man.

I sometimes pray that God will humble parents (including
stepparents) in much the same way that St. Paul was humbled on
the road to Damascus. Here was a man who had everyone afraid
of him. He had authority to imprison and kill. It wasn't until God
struck him blind and caused him to fall to the ground that Paul
became approachable. In such a dependent state, he had to rely
on anyone who would befriend him to accomplish the simplest
of tasks: using the toilet, cleaning himself, getting dressed. He
took all of these things for granted while he inflicted fear on others. Now, in humility, he reached out for help. And who did God
use to assist Paul but one of those whom Paul had come to
remove in chains. Understandably this man, Ananias, was terri-
fied, even repulsed, at the idea of approaching Paul. But, then,
God often uses the most unlikely people to help us learn about
his love.

What a blessing it might be for a stepparent to really
"need" a stepchild, to be completely dependent on that child
for a few days. How differently that relationship could take
shape around feelings of tenderness and vulnerability and
trust. Jerry had already been divorced once, and he rarely got
to see his children from his first marriage. Here was a new
opportunity to provide a young boy with a father's love, and in
turn be "saved" himself. If only his eyes had been opened as

Paul's were on that road to Damascus. Kevin was afraid, but he was ready to be Jerry's Ananias.

Kevin is fourteen and has never experienced what it feels like to relax securely in the knowledge that he is taken care of. His childhood has been filled with fear and uncertainty—no real childhood at all. The only consistent adult males in his life have all rejected him, abandoned him, and communicated by action or inaction that he is not wanted. And Kevin is angry about the rejection because somewhere deep inside he believes in himself.

From time to time in Kevin's sessions, I would sit on the floor. I wanted him to sit above me so that he wouldn't automatically feel threatened by me as an adult male. But he chose to sit on the floor as well. He wanted to be eye-to-eye. His breathing became deeper and more relaxed in this position. It was his choice to move down and be with me. Once Kevin curled up into a fetal position and cried. "This is how I feel most of the time." I cried that day, too. I felt his helplessness. And I went home exhausted. How tired must *he* be?

Kevin's mother has made some poor choices. And I wonder how I can help Kevin when his mother isn't willing to insist on some changes from Jerry. Unfortunately, Jerry grew increasingly resentful of Kevin until he exploded. It was just a matter of time. How little effort it would have taken for this man to experience and share what he himself never received—true male companionship.

Five

The Necessity
of Play

Luke, age 9

Luke was brought to my attention by his parents, who expressed concern that he did not socialize appropriately for his age and that he had a difficult time maintaining his concentration on certain tasks. Both parents were medical doctors and familiar with the possible diagnoses of ADD and ADHD. They didn't want to put him on medication except as a last resort. I agreed to see Luke, but only under the condition that both parents would also be willing to participate in counseling.

As is my usual practice, I met with both parents first to assess the history of the problem and what interventions had been attempted. Richard, his father, said that Luke has "always marched to the beat of a different drum." Ellen, Luke's mother, agreed, adding, "He's just like his father that way." At this Richard became defensive and began a noticeable oscillation between anger and withdrawal. We were no longer talking about Luke; we had issues in the marriage that needed sorting through.

Ellen said: "I think our marriage is the biggest problem. If our relationship was okay then Luke would be fine." I expressed appreciation for their (her) willingness to see a link between the marital relationship and Luke's issues, but I also wanted them to know that Luke was probably going through an individual developmental stage as well.

During the next session I spent most of my time talking with Luke. He was a playful, energetic boy. He rarely made eye contact, his mind seemed to be going a hundred miles an hour, and he would appear to act on impulse without any acknowledgment of my presence. It wasn't until I got down on the floor and started to playfully wrestle with him that Luke finally looked me in the eye—and smiled big. I had gotten his attention through play. And I wondered how often this happened at home with his father.

Luke's father was a specialist in his field. He not only practiced medicine but also engaged regularly in research and writing. His work was published extensively and he was frequently asked to speak at conferences in different countries. He was becoming a giant among his peers. The downside was that his marriage and family had suffered terribly. He was rarely at home. And when he was at home, his attention was somewhere other than with his family. "People need me," he said. "There are people who might die if not for my help." We talked about the sacrifice and potential "death" of his family.

Richard, Ellen, and Luke each needed some individual time to talk with me. Richard and Ellen recognized that something needed to change in the way the family interacted. Ellen had become chronically depressed, for which she was taking medication. Richard was aware that his absence from the family was taking a toll on everyone, including himself, but his relationship with Ellen had deteriorated to the point that he could hardly bear to be at home with her. And Luke, this great little guy, was caught in the middle of it all with his own problems. He was beginning to form nervous habits like picking his nose in public, and his classmates were making fun of him. He frequently complained of headaches and often felt too "sick" to attend school. Mom had missed a number of days from work owing to Luke's sicknesses, and she was beginning to request more help from Richard. Now Richard was beginning to miss some work, which is what finally brought them in for counseling.

I often find that one member of the family will become the "chosen one," the one through whom the family's problems manifest themselves. Severe symptoms may show up in one family member as though that one person has been secretly recruited to be the receptacle for all of the family's issues. Something was out of balance in Luke's family. Something had been left unattended in the home. And something had to give. Luke had become the rallying point for his family. It was an important role, but one that Luke was too young to understand. The important thing is that the family had come for help. I just hoped that Richard and Ellen would be willing to see the importance of their roles in providing family cohesiveness. My fear was that the parents would ask me, indirectly of course, to make them better without changing any of their behaviors. Impossible!

Luke loved to wrestle. We moved to a larger space where we could run and wrestle and play more vigorously. This was Luke's way to connect. I had no idea that therapy could be so physical. In talking with Richard I discovered that he used to be a wrestler, and a very good one at that. It just so happened that Luke had recently expressed an interest in a local wrestling club for boys his age, but he would need his father's help to participate. Richard's eyes lit up for the first time since we had begun counseling. Could this be the area of competence and connection that he was looking for with his son? He was a wizard at work, but at home he felt like a failure as both a husband and a father. Maybe wrestling would be his way back into the family. They signed up for the club.

The Three-Tiered Brain and a Place Called "Play"

A discussion of how the brain works will provide insight into ways that we can connect emotionally with our children when the busyness of life creates too much distance and stress. The key is in understanding the three-tiered brain and a place called "play."

A simplistic drawing of the brain would look like this:

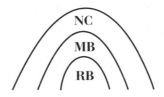

The smallest part of the brain is called the reptilian brain (RB). This is the fight-or-flight response system, the first responder in a fearful situation. This is also the part of the brain where many of us tend to spend a great deal of time, perhaps especially our children, as we are bombarded with huge amounts of information and try to survive as we move from one decision to the next.

The second tier of the brain is called the mammalian brain (MB). This is the seat of emotions, the place of nurture, comfort, empathy, and playfulness. This part of the brain performs many necessary functions. However, as we will see, it is frequently undervalued and neglected.

The third tier of the brain, the neocortex (NC), makes up about 85 percent of total brain mass. This part is associated with the functions of reason, intelligence, and creativity.

The part of the brain that I want to focus on is the second tier, the mammalian brain. Because of the deluge of information and the rapidity with which we are expected to make decisions today, I have a theory that the second tier of the brain is being neglected, especially in our children, at great cost. Cultivation of the mammalian brain requires time and attention to some of the less-valued aspects of the human character, namely playfulness and silliness. Like sleep, the time we spend in play has great reparative, restorative value. Unfortunately, our children's play is often taken too seriously. It is organized, measured, graded, rewarded. These days it seems that little emphasis is placed on just being playful for the sake of playfulness. But that is exactly what the mammalian brain requires for full development.

Some might respond: "Of course we all need downtime. That's why we take vacations." I am not referring, however, to periodic time away. Rather, I am referring to the daily need for a place called play. This is where we spend silly do-nothing time with our family that makes our sides ache from laughter. We dance, sing, play tricks, walk barefoot outside, and roll around on the floor. We learn to feel deeply and to demonstrate empathy toward others and ourselves. We move beyond the simple "how" and "what" of life to experience the "who," "why," and "when" that make life worth living. And believe it or not, this activation of the mammalian brain helps to keep the entire brain (and person) functioning well.

For a child's brain functioning to progress from the reactive, fight-or-flight level (RB) to the higher neocortex level (NC) of rational, creative thought, and to do so with genuine concern for self and others, he or she needs to cross the "mammalian bridge" to get there. If a child is to use his head and make good decisions with empathy and compassion, he needs free-form, unorganized, imaginative play. It is in this place called play, where silliness and nonsense are given expression, that a fuller movement occurs between the lower and higher brain functions. The child who neglects the experience of "play" is setting himself up (or being set up) for stress overload that will result in harmful, destructive symptoms. For men it may show up, for example, as alcoholism (or some other addiction) or as an intestinal disease such as colitis. For children it may manifest in headaches, stomachaches, emotional withdrawal, or severe acting out. It may sound funny, but if you want your child to mind and to make good decisions with compassion, then play a game.

Luke needed to find a place called play. Everything and everyone was far too serious in his life. He desired to feel deep emotional connections, especially with his father, but didn't know how to ask for them. And he wasn't old enough yet to have learned how to distract himself from his need, nor had he become sophisticated enough to mask such a need. He was just a little boy who was asking, in his own awkward way, to be taken care of, to be held and loved. He needed a place in his life where he could have fun with his family without strings of accomplishment attached. He needed to know that he was accepted and cherished for who he was in the present, not just for who he might become.

I wish I could say that Luke's parents learned to resolve problems and live with contentment together. Actually, I don't know if the marriage will survive. The hurts between Richard and Ellen have been left unattended for a long time. Each one had given up on the marriage long before coming to see me. If it hadn't been for their kids, they would have divorced already. But they stayed together, attended church every Sunday, and insisted that their kids attend Sunday school and confirmation classes. "We want them to learn about God," they explained. If only they could see themselves as the primary teachers of what it means to have a relationship with God, a relationship built on the foundation of mercy, grace, reconciliation, and forgiveness.

Luke, like many boys, needed to connect kinesthetically (through bodily movement). To reach Luke required getting down on his physical level and letting him see me play, dance, and act silly and foolish. The literal act of wrestling had become a living metaphor in this family. They needed to embrace one another in a basic, down-to-earth manner.

It is my fervent hope that all parents, and I include myself in that category, will consistently be able to see that their children have been given to them as a gift from God, and that their highest and noblest calling is to be parents. That might put me out of a job, but I think it would be worth it. It is disheartening to be led to wonder why some couples, such as Luke's parents, chose to have children in the first place, and to wonder whether I can help a child such as Luke without addressing his parents' marital discord. I can hope, through Luke and for his sake, to reach his parents' marriage. Though the burden of fixing their marriage is ultimately their responsibility and not that of their son, perhaps they will see, through him, what they need to do.

Six

A New
Move

Grant, age 11

Grant was brought to me by his parents because they needed to know that they were on the right track with their son. He didn't have any outstanding problems. In fact, he appeared to be very well adjusted for his age and stage of life. Grant, however, was a little reluctant to engage socially at school. His family had recently moved to Texas from Minnesota because of a job transfer, and he was feeling a little out of place.

Roger and Sharon, Grant's parents, had lived in Minnesota all of their lives. Both still had family there, including both sets of grandparents. Everyone had a difficult time with the decision to move because their support system in Minnesota was so strong. Grant saw each of his grandparents at least once a week, and there were several cousins to play with who were close in age. Now the family was starting over in a new place, and Grant's parents were questioning whether they had done the right thing.

We discussed the positives of the original decision to move, as a way to develop a more balanced picture of the situation. The job transfer was a move up in the company with more opportunities for advancement. The economy had begun to slow when Roger accepted the offer to move, and he was transferring into a stronger market. Back in Minnesota Sharon had to work part-time for the family to make ends meet. With this move, Sharon could now be a stay-at-home mom again (they had two other children, ages 7 and 4), which is something everyone wanted.

Obviously this family was grieving the loss of a significant support system. Even though the gains were substantial, the trade-offs were deeply felt and would need to be addressed successfully for everyone to achieve contentment. Sharon appeared to be the most anxious of all, and she especially needed to become more settled.

Roger was busy proving himself in a new position, and had a built-in support system on the job. The children had the structure of school, with opportunities to develop new friendships. Sharon, however, did not have an immediate outlet for socialization, and was feeling alone and disconnected. The referral to me for counseling came through a secretary at the church office where their youngest was enrolled in preschool. The family did not attend church, but they had no other referral source to consult for counseling and seemed grateful that such services were available.

I visited with Grant a couple of times so that I could give his parents feedback on my observations. Basically Grant was doing fine. His grades were good, he didn't get into trouble, and he seemed cheerful and playful in my presence. Roger and Sharon, especially Sharon, needed reassurance that they were good parents. They had never experienced such doubts before, but this move had shaken their confidence.

One of the tools that I use with parents in transition is a diagnostic review of the emotional care of their children. The most effective review that I have found is drawn from a book by Dorothy Walter Baruch. Written in 1949, Baruch's review offers a clear and concise picture of emotional needs that can lie at the heart of disciplinary problems. Baruch asks, "What are the basic emotional requirements that must come to every small infant, to every growing child, to every adult?" She identifies five key needs:

1. Affection: "Real down-to-earth, sincere loving."
2. Knowledge of belonging: "The glow of knowing oneself to be a part of some bigger whole."
3. Pleasure that comes through the senses: "The hearty enjoyment of touch and taste and smell" and so on.
4. Sense of achievement: The conviction that he or she is "adequate to meet life's demands," together with the knowledge that achievements are recognized.
5. Acceptance and understanding: "The deep relief of knowing that we can be ourselves with honest freedom."

(*New Ways in Discipline*, pp. 13-14)

I have come to see that an important part of my work with parents is to provide reassurance. Baruch's list of emotional needs invites parents to evaluate themselves and their families; usually, after using this information as a checklist, parents I work with feel encouraged. In our mobile society, parents have an increasing need to hear from a professional that they are good parents and on the right track. Grant's parents fit this profile. They didn't need long-term counseling. They needed a new support system.

I happened to be familiar with the church and preschool where Sharon had received the referral. A play group met there once-a-week, and a woman led a fellowship and Bible study for stay-at-home moms another day of the week. I encouraged Sharon to inquire about these activities. She did so. After a few weeks of interaction with these other moms, the family decided to start attending church at the same place. When they followed up with me for counseling, Roger and Sharon reported feeling more at ease with their move and encouraged by how well the kids were adjusting, including Grant.

Grant was initially presented as the focal point of concern. However, as so often happens, I quickly discovered that what we had in front of us was a larger family concern: a new state, a new house, a new job, a new school, the loss of a support system, the loss of familiar stores, doctors, history, and community resources. I don't think we ever anticipate just how significantly our lives will change when we consider a move. Roger and Sharon were doing what they thought was best for their family in the long run, but the immediate changes would require all of their personal emotional resources.

Sometimes I think parents need permission to put their own oxygen mask on before they attend to their children, like the directions given by a flight attendant. Parents need to make sure they are taking care of their own emotional needs so they can better help and support their children during times of transition and crisis. Good self-care is different from selfishness. A parent can only give that which he or she has received. In other words, it's hard to give support when you don't feel supported yourself.

I believe the church has a wonderful opportunity today in our faster-growing population centers. People are moving to cities and suburbs, away from their primary support systems. Churches could establish "transition ministries" in which people could network and receive education regarding local schools, medical services, shopping, Christian bookstores, and yes, worship opportunities. Play groups, men's breakfasts, new-baby support groups, couples' dinner clubs—anything is possible in the formation of our faith communities. As a counselor, I know that people generally achieve and maintain better health when they are socially connected in a supportive community. Churches can make an important contribution through programs such as these.

This particular chapter has taken us in a little different direction from the rest of the book. I have attempted to speak more broadly by considering the needs of families who are on the move. Without a doubt, our children will feel supported, secure, nurtured, and confident to the extent that parents feel the same. In fact, it just might be that one of the best ways for us to tell our children that we love them is by taking better care of ourselves first.

Men Who
Are Just
Like Me

Introduction
to Adult
Males

The profiles in this book provide a glimpse of the issues each of the boys may have to face in adulthood. Each one will need to overcome significant emotional deficits if he is going to enjoy relational satisfaction in marriage and family. In many ways, getting older provides more sophisticated avenues for deflecting or masking emotional deficits.

I would like to begin this section by encouraging men who need help in their personal lives not to hesitate in seeking it. Allow me to draw a parallel by way of my brother-in-law Joe. Joe is the stepfather to my nephew and niece. He does a good job of honoring their biological father's role in their lives, while always making himself available to the kids whenever they need him. He works hard as the owner of an auto mechanic shop, even long hours at different times and seasons, but makes his family (the whole family) a priority. It is this sense of priority that determines much of his schedule. He has had the opportunity to participate in activities such as assisting with a NASCAR racing team (and could easily "justify" it as important to his professional development), but this would take him away from his family. His family is much more important to him than the personal achievement he would feel on the road. In other words, his "success" as a man revolves primarily around his relationship with his family.

I remember when I first began to realize that Joe and I were in the same line of work, he as a mechanic and I as a counselor. He was talking about how people came to him with their cars only after they had attempted a number of things to correct the problem and had finally decided to seek professional help. The hope of each person who walks through his door is that Joe will find something minor, even free, to correct the problem. Just a turn of a screw here or a missing cap there and, voila, it's done. Painless! Although some things are relatively minor to repair, he says that frequently he has to help the person through a grieving process that includes denial, anger, depression (obviously on a smaller scale than therapy, but still a form of helplessness), and eventually acceptance. Even though the car was slipping badly, pulling sharply, burning oil quickly, or exhibiting some other symptoms, the reality of losing more time and money than expected takes a while to digest.

Once Joe convinces the customer to leave the car for repair, he sets out to more fully diagnose the problem(s). He drives the car to see how it feels. He lifts the hood to listen carefully to how the engine runs. He considers the history of the car, such as its mileage, make, and model, and searches a database for what other mechanics have discovered to be the problem according to related symptoms. Once he has an idea, hunch, or theory, he decides on an intervention that will be the least costly and works his way up from there. When he identifies an area to address, he calls the customer and requests permission to proceed. After all, the customer is the one paying for it; he needs to be a part of the decision-making process. Even when the customer decides to proceed and knows how much the cost will be, he may still express disappointment and anger toward Joe. And if Joe suggests different behaviors for driving the car to keep it in good repair, the customer might express resentment instead of appreciation for the insight.

Sometimes men bring their cars to Joe expressing disappointment in themselves for not being able to fix their cars, as though it was a skill that should come naturally to them. For some men it almost seems like a mark of shame not to be able to fix their own car. Joe puts them at ease by saying that cars are more difficult today, with computers and all, and that most people can't fix their own cars anymore. This expression of "normalcy" seems reassuring to the men who leave their cars for another man to fix.

The parallels between Joe the mechanic and Rick the counselor are striking. We go through many of the same steps, right down to dealing with insurance companies for some of the work. However, I sometimes envy my brother-in-law because his interventions are much more straightforward. Unlike counseling, Joe can diagnose a problem, replace a part, and have the car running again. At times a relatively simple behavioral change will yield a large improvement in counseling, but more often than not, the process is far more idiosyncratic. In other words, each person and situation is a little different. People don't roll off an assembly line.

I share this comparison as a way of encouraging men to seek help when they need it. Going to a counselor is a mark of resourcefulness and strength, not personal failure. Why do we think that we should automatically know how to repair our lives? Our personal selves are much more complex than a car. We eventually seek out professional help to keep our vehicles in good running order. We owe it to ourselves and our families to do the same when our inner lives are out of order.

As we move into the section on adult males, I hope to demonstrate that those who sit before me are God's children who have unfinished business—the business of embracing the fact that God intends to work in and through our lives to help us attain increased health and wholeness. I attempt to identify with each man on some level, and so I have titled this section "Men Who Are Just Like Me." It is easy to carry unrealistic expectations into my sessions with these men. I try to avoid this by reminding myself that as a man myself, I share in their struggles. And in the end, I know that each man needs to hear the same voice that I long for, the one that tells me, "I love you, Son."

Seven

Self-Doubt

Jim, age 36

Jim was one of my first male clients when I began working as a pastoral counselor. He was a white, thirty-six-year-old single male who still lived at home with his parents. He was also in a great deal of emotional and psychic pain. His father had physically and verbally abused him for as long as he could remember. A priest, one of the few men he trusted as a young boy, had sexually molested him. Like his father, Jim was an alcoholic. He had been sober for three months when he came to see me.

I could see right away that Jim felt both frightened and ashamed. He deeply desired to be embraced by someone, anyone, but at the same time he was desperately afraid of being seen. I knew it would be easy to lose Jim as a client. In fact, I had rarely seen an alcoholic make it without at least trading one addiction for another. But Jim had definitely hit bottom, and had actually sought me out on his own without a court order or an ultimatum from a family member, employer, or friend. He was simply tired of making good starts only to hit the wall halfway into his journey on the newest "right path."

"I'm thirty-six years old, and either I need to make a lasting change or give up and die."

Whenever Jim talked about his nightmares (which were always about running away from someone who was chasing him), despair would fill the room. Some days the burden felt so great to me that I didn't know if I could bear to be in the same room with him. Sometimes he couldn't make it for counseling, and I actually felt relieved (and ashamed for feeling that way). He frequently hung his head, plagued by the feeling that he would never be free of self-images imposed by his father, negative images reinforced by words like "stupid," "idiot," and "failure." It didn't matter what Jim accomplished, he would always see himself as incompetent and a failure. He turned to me for help in looking at himself and life differently: with hope.

Jim had grown up in a lower-middle-income, blue-collar family. His dad worked in factories and drank himself to sleep every night, while his mother picked up part-time jobs and smoked like a chimney. Their house was small and unkempt. Dogs and cats had free rein in the place, and meals were unpredictable. The kids were on their own from a very young age. Now that Jim was attempting to move from a factory setting to a professional computer-technician trade, he severely doubted that he had what it would take just on a social, verbal level. He had grown up and worked in environments in which a small provocation could be sufficient grounds for a physical fight. "I would just kick his ass," Jim said as he reflected on past disagreements with coworkers. But he realized that this would not fly in an office setting, which added to his doubts about his ability to succeed.

We instituted a plan of treatment that included weekly attendance at Alcoholics Anonymous meetings, a psychiatric evaluation for depression, and weekly counseling sessions. Jim not only made a good start but also remained on track and continued to be sober and productive. He went to college for a two-year computer certificate. I was very proud of him. Jim also helped me—

though without knowing it—as I began to take a closer look at some unattended areas of my own life.

As I listened to Jim, I was reminded of how for years my father would suggest that I get a factory job. In fact, I can remember being in my last year of college (something no one in my dad's immediate family had ever accomplished) and expressing doubts about what my career path would be. My dad's response? "Factories have always been good to me. You can get a job and be productive. Don't spend any more money or time on school. Look where it's gotten you so far. By your age I . . ." So how did I respond to his advice? I went on to graduate and obtain two more degrees. Respect at last from my father? Not until I actually started making money. I sure worked hard for his approval and respect. Jim and I were much closer than I wanted to imagine.

The desire and need for a father's blessing is inherent and powerful. As male-studies researcher Samuel Osherson explains, the very foundation of who we are as men is directly related to this blessing:

> Often we find a sense of worth as men only in living up, proving we are smart enough for teachers, tough enough for coaches, and loyal enough for bosses.
>
> Since many men don't get a blessing from the male community, they aren't always sure if they really and truly have the right stuff. This is the core sense of male shame (*Wrestling with Love*, p. 84).

Jim harbored a tremendous amount of anger toward his father, and he needed to work through it. I asked him to write a letter to his father. I told him to imagine that his father had died and that he had asked Jim to write to him and express his most honest thoughts and feelings about their relationship. I often find that having the client imagine the recipient is dead allows more genuine emotion to come forth. Sometimes this approach gives the author of the letter an opportunity to adopt a more objective view of the recipient, a necessary part of the healing process.

> Dad,
>
> I am writing this letter because you are gone now. I never had the opportunity to tell you how I felt. At an early age in my life, I looked up to you and thought you were the best guy in the world. It's been a long time since I felt that way. You always made me feel like a piece of shit in your eyes, everything that I've done was wrong. You were supposed to teach me about life and how to do things. Instead, when I tried to do things, you would put me down, call me stupid, retarded, or useless. That's the way I felt most of the time, that I am useless and not worth anything. I've been living my life scared. I wanted to do many things with my life but am too insecure to try them, in fear of being laughed at or failing. Dad, you've done a lot of terrible things to us — Mom and my brothers and sisters. That is hard to forgive you for. We grew up in a very unsafe environment; we withstood the physical abuse, but the mental abuse lives on with us forever. I am not saying you did not care for us. You always provided a place to live, food, and clothes, and worked hard to do that. But you failed us in the most important way, which is love and understanding, and teaching us how to have confidence. And that when we failed at something, it was not the end of the world, but to believe in ourselves and keep trying. One year ago I was trying to improve my education. You came in drunk and in a bad mood, and told me again that I was worthless and no good, that I should have finished school ten years ago. You took away that little bit of confidence I had left.
>
> Jim

After Jim read the letter aloud in my presence, I asked him if he felt more like hugging his father or hitting him. "Hitting him," he said. "I hate my father." And I realized that Jim might never enjoy a good relationship with his earthly father.

I wanted Jim to experience the same healing love of God, his heavenly father, that I have felt in my life. We discussed prayer and the idea of "God at work" in his life. An important part of our conversation centered around the suffering of God's son (though I cringed a little inside as I realized that this is an image of a father sacrificing his son; I dared not mention Abraham and Isaac). But Jim was resistant. His only contact with the church had included a harsh Catholic school and molestation by a priest. How could I ask him to trust in God? Maybe I couldn't. Perhaps I simply needed to demonstrate a male relationship that could be trusted.

I felt confused by my identity as a "pastoral" counselor. After all, I was supposed to lead others to their ultimate healing in Christ. Then I remembered how Jesus spent endless hours with his disciples long before they understood who he was. Eventually Jesus asked his disciples, "Who do you say that I am?" And Peter responded, "You are the Christ" (Mark 8:29). Peter got the answer right. Then he went on to deny Jesus three times. But Jesus never gave up on Peter. I dared not convey a sense of disappointment in Jim for not agreeing with my theology. After all, God is more than my theology.

Jim had been denied the opportunity to form trusting relationships at an early age. He lived with mental and emotional anguish and had found pseudorelief in a bottle. "Hitting bottom" was no longer an option for Jim. He lived on the bottom.

A small spark of belief in his intrinsic worth had all but flickered out in Jim. He was looking for a man that he could trust with his life's stories—someone who would respect and not despise or shame him. Jim already felt betrayed by God. I just hope he can begin to see God's love for him through me, even if he doesn't initially recognize this love as coming from God.

Eight

Infidelity

Mark, age 40

Mark was about to turn forty when he and his wife came to see me for counseling. It had recently come to light that Mark had been having an affair with a coworker, a subordinate in his law firm. His wife, Jill, was understandably distraught. Could the marriage survive this revelation? Mark was depressed and confused. And more than anything he wanted to save his marriage. Their two children were young enough that they really couldn't understand what was happening in the family. As long as Mommy and Daddy were together, they would be fine.

Jill had been deeply betrayed by Mark and didn't know if she would ever trust him again. She wanted some time away from Mark. They arranged a temporary separation, with Mark securing an apartment. I scheduled both individual and marital counseling for this couple. They were both in a great deal of pain.

Mark was a successful partner in a large law firm. He frequently spent several days at a time trying cases away from home, and it was under these circumstances that the affair had occurred. His legal cases were demanding. They required long hours of preparation and intense negotiation. Mark had reached the height of his career at a relatively young age. He worked hard, driving himself to push beyond his previous limits. He was energized by the "game," the "kill," the "win." He was good at what he did, and he knew it.

When Mark was growing up, his father's commitment to his work had caused him to be physically and emotionally absent from his wife and children. In addition, Mark's father had had affairs. Mark was aware of the similarities between himself and his father, but up to this point had consoled himself with the fact that he had at least been faithful to his wife. Now that was no longer true, and Mark had lost touch with his true self.

As Mark and I began to review his life and recover some of his earliest delights and dreams as a young college student, we discovered that Mark had for a long time perceived himself to be on a spiritual journey. He loved philosophy, religion, and reading fiction, and had been drawn to explore his relationship with God at an early age. He had always wanted to be a good husband and father and to teach his children by example how to live a Christian life. But somewhere along the way he took a wrong turn. Somehow he got off track. And he wondered whether he could ever "go back."

Our true self can be suppressed early on in the face of societal demands for certain types of so-called masculinity. Researchers Deborah David and Robert Brannon have identified four stereotyped male images that seem to be prevalent in our society. Aspects of each of these four images can be seen in Mark's experience as well as those of the other men and boys portrayed in this book. Most importantly, these four types of masculinity feed into the disconnection between a man's head and his heart. William S. Pollack summarizes David and Brannon's four images as follows:

The injunction to become a Sturdy Oak refers to men's stoicism: We teach little boys not to share pain or openly grieve. The Give 'em Hell stance of our sports coaches creates the false self of daring, bravado, and love for violence, while the ideal of being a Big Wheel stresses the need to achieve status and power at any cost. But perhaps the most traumatizing, straitjacketing social role training is that No Sissy Stuff—the condemnation of the expression in boys of any strong, dependent, or warm feelings or urges that are seen as feminine and therefore as totally unacceptable or even taboo. . . . The "daddy with no feelings, work til you drop" track for men begins long before the work-career ladder is in view ("No Man Is an Island: Toward a New Psychoanalytic Psychology of Men," in *A New Psychology of Men*, edited by Ronald F. Levant and William S. Pollack, p. 44).

An important part of my discussion with Mark centered around the disconnection he had experienced between his head and his heart. His work required him to focus so intensely on the intellectual part of his life that he had not attended to the emotional part. But as he soon came to understand, the emotions don't go away. They just go underground, and become increasingly vulnerable to an unexpected seduction. This is not to say that Mark was passive and helpless in his betrayal of himself, his wife and family, and God—far from it. But he was vulnerable. He had lost track of his good senses. He was going full throttle at a hundred miles an hour, and nothing could get in his way—except himself. And he fell hard!

As Mark retold the story of how he gave in to temptation and now desperately desired to recover Jill's trust, I felt myself flinch inside emotionally. I was simultaneously being pulled toward righteous indignation and empathy. I knew the empathy needed to win out (mercy is greater than judgment), but I was dealing with a factor that cut close to my own heart and mind: my own fear of temptation.

I remembered a time when I was vulnerable with a new client. By God's grace I didn't succumb to my own sexual appetites, but I could have. I had allowed plenty of room for the thoughts and feelings to grow in my mind and heart. I looked forward to seeing this woman in counseling, not for the purpose of helping her but simply to be with her. I double-checked the way that I dressed and looked before seeing her. I felt anxious if she was late or missed an appointment. Fortunately I noticed early on that these thoughts and behaviors were out of whack. I discussed my vulnerability with a couple of colleagues, my accountability group, who promptly agreed that I needed to terminate the relationship. I said good-bye to the woman at the next session. Reflecting on this experience, I found empathy for Mark.

Mark agonized over his fallen state. He had broken his commitment to Jill, to God, and to himself. We talked about how his father's work caused him to be physically and emotionally distant from the family, and I encouraged him to write a letter. As I had with Jim, I asked Mark to write a letter from the perspective that his father had died after asking for an honest accounting of their relationship.

Dear Dad,

I sometimes look at my own two sons and recall that I was once a little boy too—innocent, naïve, and curious about the world. Who would have imagined then what I would become? Certainly not me. I had no map, no plan, no compass. You, I suspect, neither saw enough potential to allow you even to begin to imagine the successes I would achieve nor, I doubt, the flaws in character that would allow me to sink so low. How could you have imagined these things when you did not know me? Perhaps the distance between us made it that much more difficult for me to know and define myself.

I do not mean to suggest that you are somehow responsible for the situation in which I now find myself. I realize that I alone am responsible for my actions and for the pain that I have caused Jill — for what I have done and for what I have left undone.

Still, as I struggle to understand my own failings, I cannot help but reflect on you, on your limitations as a parent and as a husband, and grieve for the relationship that we never had. There is no point now in reciting every instance or characteristic that defined you as a parent. That is in the past. In the end, the most bitter disappointment was that even in your later years, you made no effort to make the best of the days that remained, or even to acknowledge the reality of the past. Perhaps now that you are in God's hands, you see these things, and I in turn can accept your weaknesses, acknowledge your human limitations, and forgive you. I have always loved you.

As for myself, I have thought from time to time that I have a destiny in this world, that some great and important unknown thing awaited me. I see now that, God and Jill willing, my primary goal on earth is simple — to be the best husband for Jill and father for Eric, Catherine, and Trent that I can be. I have found my compass, am figuring out the map, and am working on a plan.

From the beginning of time we have been warned to appreciate what we have. Like Eve of the Old Testament, Mr. Scrooge from A Christmas Carol, and Dorothy from The Wizard of Oz, I have learned some of life's most important, simple, and elegant lessons from this experience. Unlike Dorothy, though, tapping my heels together cannot save me or repair the damage I have done. I have made my peace with God. I can only hope and pray that with a great deal of hard work and time, Jill and I can heal.

Love,
Your Son

Mark has done some significant soul-searching throughout his ordeal. Some men never face their true selves. It's just too frightening. But Mark knows what's important on the levels of both the head and the heart. He has found a place of true remorse. His marriage may have a chance for survival and renewal because Mark allowed himself to be humbled by his weaknesses. (St. Paul said in 2 Corinthians 12:10, "When I am weak, then I [through God] am strong.") We pray for God's grace to intervene in this marriage.

So many of us, men and women, view life as being separated into compartments—mind and body, work and home—as if these aspects of life can ever be truly separated. "Don't bring your work home, and don't bring your home to work" is an unwritten rule of life. And we pay dearly for this division. Mark had no pictures of his family at work, he rarely mentioned his wife and kids at the office, and he never invited them to see him at work. Further, he didn't share his work in conversation at home, even though wireless technology kept him at work while he was physically at home. Work and home were two separate worlds that could never meet. No wonder he convinced himself that he could live a different life at work. (Suggestion: If your workplace environment does not encourage and support a high view of marriage and family, then you're probably working in the wrong place.)

I am reminded of "men of faith" from the Bible. Such men as Samson and David are good examples. If we read only the parts of their stories in which God demonstrates his power (as in a child's introductory version of the Bible), we could easily fail to see that these men of great conviction and faith in God were also men who fell hard owing to their weakness and sinfulness: Samson with Delilah, David with Bathsheba. Oh, how the mighty do fall. These were men of extraordinary abilities. These were men who genuinely knew God's presence and power in their lives. But these were also men who knew the loneliness and darkness that comes with betraying God, self, and others. With just a few moments of passion, everything began to crumble. They had no way to turn back the clock. The damage was done. (Lord, have mercy on us.)

Mark had been blessed with many material and social advantages while growing up. He had also spent a good part of his life trying to gain his absent father's approval. Mark followed in his father's absentee footsteps, but had consoled himself with the thought that even if he wasn't always present for his own family, at least he was faithful. Now even that was gone.

God was stirring in Mark's heart. Mark had known the tenderness of God's grace, and he wondered if he could ever experience that feeling of assurance again. By God's grace and intervention, he prayed for the healing of his family. However, in a very real way, he understood that he needed to know God's healing work in his own life first. Fortunately, Mark was humble enough to accept full responsibility for his actions. And he no longer took for granted the purpose of his life as husband and father.

Mark was seeking continuity between head, heart, and hands. He wanted to feel whole and honest. He took some comfort in seeing God demonstrate mercy toward men of faith in the Bible who had fallen. He also observed that God's mercy doesn't mitigate the painful consequences of sin. Through it all Mark discovered that in the midst of his greatest weakness God could intervene and give him strength where none had existed before. Mark truly heard the voice of his heavenly father speak a word of tenderness and love toward him as his dear son.

Nine

Divorce

Steven, age 39

When Steven came to see me, he had been divorced for about two years. His wife of eleven years came home one day to say she didn't love him anymore and was moving in with another man, whom she subsequently married. Steven was devastated. He had grown up in a stable middle-income home: traditional, conservative, and religious. Marriage was supposed to be sacred and "till death we do part." Now, two years after the divorce, he was suffering from increasingly frequent depressive episodes. He was even having thoughts of suicide, and just didn't want to continue with life the way he was feeling.

Steven was a bright and gifted man. He was musically talented and worked as a minister of music at a local church. He gave piano lessons for children. He had always imagined himself serving the Lord in such a capacity, but with all his self-doubt he was beginning to lose the joy he had once found in his work. He was lonely, empty, and afraid that he would never enjoy a close, intimate relationship again.

I really enjoyed my conversations with Steven. He was sensitive and witty. And he shared a vulnerability with me that made me wish our relationship had not been formed around my role as a counselor. In other words, I sometimes wanted to be his friend more than his counselor. But I knew that I could wear only one hat, and he was requesting help from me because I was a counselor. So I remembered my responsibility to keep the boundaries clear.

One of the things that I noticed about Steven was that whenever he shared a vulnerability, such as fear, disappointment, or loss, he soon after began talking philosophically and filling the room with intellectualizations. Then he quickly shifted the conversation to some aspect of competency in his work, even wanting to give me printouts of his musical accomplishments. I came to recognize this as a stabilizing pattern for Steven. Weakness had to be balanced by strength.

This shift between weakness and strength was familiar to me in my work with men. And I had certainly participated in such a balancing act myself. After all, as men we are taught to show no fear and that big boys don't cry. If we just work hard enough, we will succeed to the point that we will never have to rely on anyone but ourselves. Self-sufficiency is the name of the game. What a bunch of garbage!

Herbert Anderson is a professor of psychology who has tied together the concepts of vulnerability, loss, grief, and cultural myths for men in a type of internal, emotional flinch response:

> In order to avoid acknowledging neediness, men flinch from the connections they want when loss occurs. When they do, they reinforce the common myth that grown men have little to offer one another in times of emotional need. . . .
>
> The cultural myth supporting the idea men should not be vulnerable probably has the most power to determine male response to loss. If it is not masculine to be vulnerable, then

men will spend time and energy and sometimes considerable money to eliminate vulnerability, that is, their susceptibility to being wounded ("Men and Grief: The Hidden Sea of Tears without Outlet," in *The Care of Men,* edited by Christie Cozad Neuger and James Newton Poling, pp. 210-211).

Steven cried in my presence, and I saw tenderness and grace. But why did Steven cry for the first time only after reflecting on his father's death? What about the pain of his divorce? So many men seem to touch the reservoir of tears, finally, around the issue of their father's deteriorating health and death. Indeed, whenever Steven talked about the pain of his divorce, the death of his father was not far behind. How deeply one loss touches another. Steven was twenty-six when his father died suddenly of heart failure. I asked him to write a letter.

Dear Dad,

I think about you often, almost every day. I guess I can only imagine how Mom misses you also. You were both obviously very much in love, and that alone has, by example, taught me a lot about how to live and love. You taught me a lot about commitment from your relationship to Mom, to the church, to God, to your children. All of these relationships were so solid and strong, dependable and unshakable that it seems almost impossible for anyone (myself included) to live up to those standards. I sometimes think that I expected this kind of deep commitment from Lisa, unrealistically. How could I criticize you for being too committed? . . . Yet sometimes I find everyone else to be too slack, too uncommitted, making me feel put upon by these expectations, set up for discontent. Did you feel that way? Did people used to display more commitment? You rarely displayed frustration to us kids. How did you deal with unmet expectations? Did you have unmet expectations? I am sorry that I did not mature enough while you were alive to ask these questions . . . to know that we are more alike than different, so you might have the wisdom of experience to offer me. I think I was still convinced that we were completely different at the time of your death. I miss your wisdom that I did have the sense to ask for. Your ideas for working and dealing with people were always clear, fair, and correct. I am not good at dealing with individuals, and wish I could have mined your experiences more.

I find myself regularly saying the funny sayings that you always said, and which I thought were silly. No one can ever mention hail (as in weather) without me either saying or thinking, "The hail you say." There are a million more of your sayings that are now carried on by me, and probably only endured by others (they may find themselves saying them some day too). I am glad that you did not have to see me get divorced, but I know you would have offered some helpful ideas, and I am worse off for not having them.

I think you would be disappointed in how my life has turned out. I used to tell myself that I would never stay in a situation in which work was a major stress (like I think it was for you). Now I believe that I am in that situation, following in your footsteps, headed for an early death after a tense life. It still seems like the best thing I could do would be to not follow in your footsteps; to step away from pressures and relax, starting over with more joy, love, and pleasure, and learning to avoid the killer stress and tension.

I love you and I miss you,

Steven

Steven has been blessed with some very good memories of his father. He remembers consistency in his parents' relationship, a stable and expressive religious upbringing, and his father's determination to care and provide for his family. Steven obviously loves and misses his father—if only he could have been here for him during his divorce, maybe he could have helped—but Steven was now "headed for an early death after a tense life."

The picture of Steven's father that takes shape is one of a man who felt stuck in his work, trying to make the best of a stressful situation. He had bills to pay and mouths to feed. And this was a man who loved his wife and children, who enjoyed a hearty laugh and had a good sense of humor. This was also a man of faith and conviction in his relationship with God, who was happy to discuss his beliefs and religious practices with others. Unfortunately, he died before Steven was old enough to more fully appreciate him.

I find myself drawn to Steven's curiosity about whether his father had any unmet expectations. I can't help but wonder whether Steven's father ever demonstrated vulnerability and brokenness in his presence. What about the stress? What about the tension? Why is Steven so unsure about whether his father had any unmet expectations? Of course he did! Steven had only an image of his father's competency. But what of his failures? Did his father's personal view of the Christian life include a place for interpersonal confession? As the Apostle James wrote, "Confess your sins to each other . . . so that you may be healed" (James 5:16). How tragic it is for our children when we show them only the competent side of our lives. How untouchable we must be. What a lost opportunity for healing—emotional, physical, spiritual, relational.

I sometimes think that we as men make the mistake of assuming that if we show our weaknesses to our children, they will use it as an excuse for bad behavior, or worse, they will lose respect for us. We fail to recognize that the mark of Christian leadership has nothing to do with how strong or capable we are, but rather how fully we can acknowledge our need for God's mercy and grace. What a comfort it is to hear St. Paul express his own personal faith struggles, "What I want to do I do not do, but what I hate I do" (Romans 7:15). It's where he ends up that makes all the difference: "When I am weak, then I [through God] am strong" (2 Corinthians 12:10). It just might be that the most helpful way we can demonstrate our love to our sons is by sharing our weaknesses with them.

Ten

Sexual Addiction and the Cycle of Grief

Sam, age 43

Sam came to me after five years of an increasingly debilitating sexual addiction. It started with the Internet and developed from there. Now his wife, Carol, was on the verge of leaving him and taking their three children with her. Sam saw counseling as his last hope.

At least half the men that I see in counseling struggle with sexual addictions. These days it often starts with surfing the Internet for pornography. Sometimes these men even spend extra time at work viewing these sites (not realizing or caring that their viewing habits are likely being documented by employers who are concerned about liability issues). Like drug addictions, sexual addictions are progressive. Eventually these men move from passive viewing to Internet chat.

Sam had followed this very course of addictive behavior, requiring progressively more frequent and intense pornographic material to satisfy him. Finally he began chatting online with a person he believed to be a woman. Their conversations grew increasingly graphic. They discussed their own marriages and personal discontent. This fantasy-driven "conversation" eventually included discussion of the possibility that the two of them meet. This never materialized, but it came close.

In addition, business associates encouraged Sam to attend men's clubs with them. "It's part of doing business," they said. "After all, it's not like you're being unfaithful—just a little innocent fun. Besides, the food is great! It loosens clients up an they feel more like closing the deal." When Sam asked what the other men's wives thought about them going to these clubs, they all responded that their wives didn't care. "You can look, but don't touch, that's their attitude," Sam was told. Of course, a little lap dance now and then was okay, as long as you don't tell the wife. After all, the men still had their clothes on, and it was a public (socially sanctioned) activity—right?

Sam's wife grew increasingly uncomfortable with his sexual interests. She found pornographic videos he had purchased, as well as a copy of Internet correspondence from one of his chat sessions. But Carol was very insecure, and her first line of defense was to compete with her husband's fantasies rather than confront his illness.

One day, though, Carol found a box of condoms in Sam's coat. She remained silent for a long time, afraid of what she might hear if she asked Sam to explain. Finally, she confronted him. He told her he just wanted to be prepared when he went out of town on business in case something happened. She was furious and hurt. She felt betrayed and rejected. Over the next several weeks and months, she shifted between intense anger and withdrawal. Finally she gave Sam an ultimatum: Get help or the marriage is over. After responding with intense anger, Sam finally came to seek help.

Carol had initially seemed willing to put up with a little of Sam's addictive behavior, but eventually it became intolerable. I was reminded of the story of Abraham and Sarah in the Old Testament. Because Sarah was unable to bear children and because the couple desired to continue the family lineage, Sarah suggested that Abraham have a child by a concubine. Seemed simple enough. After all, such a solution was socially and legally acceptable under the circumstances. So Abraham went ahead with the plan. And what was Sarah's response to the concubine and her son by Abraham? Disgust! Sure, Sarah had encouraged it, but the hurtful reality of the experience didn't match the social and legal acceptability. No amount of sanctioning could remove the pain of betrayal.

I always have to be careful when I work with a sexually addicted person. It's easy for my own self-righteousness to flare up, especially when children are involved and divorce is a real threat. Part of me just wants to shake the man and say, "Wake up!" But, then, maybe he is in the process of waking up. Maybe this counseling is a welcome opportunity for him to finally begin to address his illness. Or is it that I'm afraid of what I see in myself as I sit before this man? How far have my own fantasies gone? But for the grace of God . . .

I remember one especially intense work period when I was burning the candle at both ends. I wasn't paying enough attention to my wife and family and feeling rather disconnected. This also happened to be a time when I was seeing an unusually large number of sexually addicted men in counseling. One night I decided, out of curiosity, to surf the Web "just a little" to see what these men were looking at. It was easy. All I did was put in the word "sex" or "pornography" and I was on my way. The pictures became increasingly intense, and many were free and uncensored. It was, I must admit, sexually arousing, and I remained on-line longer than I had intended. Some time later the words of St. Paul came to mind, "If you think you are standing firm, be careful that you don't fall" (1 Corinthians 10:12). Perhaps I wouldn't go into my next counseling session with as much self-righteousness as I had before.

Sam and I talked about his parents' relationship as a way to understand some of his own relational decisions in his marriage. Sam began to cry as he talked about his father, who had died several years earlier. I requested he write a letter to his father.

My Dearest Father,

When I was growing up you were there, but I cannot remember when you were not intoxicated to some degree. I know that you would brew coffee in the morning and I would awake to the wonderful smell. I would come into the kitchen and you would be drinking coffee as a medicine for the hangover you were suffering from the night before. I see that now as an adult looking back, not as a child loving his father. I do not understand that you could not see the damage you were doing to yourself, Mom, and me. Why did you turn to alcohol instead of the Lord or Mom? I wish I had that answer, because you really screwed up your life and mine in the process. If you had the guts to face your problems instead of turning to the bottle, my life probably would be very different today. I would have realized that my beautiful wife needed me for many things besides just a paycheck.

The Lord teaches that forgiveness is divine, and I do forgive you with all my heart, but I am mad that you did not think enough of yourself or your family to stop or even to look for treatment for your problems. Mom and I needed you so much to be strong, and you got your strength from alcohol. The many lessons that I learned from my growing up really screwed up my life. The distance that was between Mom and you rubbed off into my marriage, and I could not see it because I thought it was "normal" behavior.

I pray to the Lord that he will come into my life and my marriage each moment of each day and give us the healing that we both need so desperately. My wife cannot bear to make love to me without wanting to

run away and hide. All I ever wanted to do was love her and take care
of her, but all I have done is destroy the most precious person in my life.
Things that I thought or was brought up to think were "normal" are
really un-Christian behavior. A more Christian environment would have
made many differences in my life.

I am going to say good-bye for now. You and Mom are always in
my heart and in my prayers. I pray that you and Mom are in heaven
where you belong and not apart. I also pray that God and counseling
can help me deal with the issues that you and I have outstanding. I
really do love you despite what I may have written, for a child will
always love his parents no matter what. I just wish you had taken the
right path and made the right decisions in your life, because it could
have been much better for the both of us.

Your loving son, always and forever,

Sam

I wish Sam had come to see me five years earlier. But, then, he couldn't see *himself* five years ago. How tragic it is when a person who has tenderness in his heart for what is right chooses to live so far over the edge. Was he living with such a warped sense of normal that he didn't know how harmful his behaviors were to his wife and children? Denial is a powerful thing. Can he honestly blame his father for his own personal failures? Perhaps that's part of the journey toward self-discovery.

As I listened to Sam read his letter aloud, I was struck by his recognition that "my beautiful wife needed me for many things besides just a paycheck." He was beginning to get closer to the meaning of intimacy. He saw the absence of emotional presence in his father's distant, self-medicated life. And now he has repeated this theme, with a different form of addiction, in his own family. We talked about what his children might say about him as they sit with me twenty years from now in counseling. Once again he saw himself in his father. As with so many of us men, Sam's self-worth was defined by his roles as protector and provider instead of as a reassuring emotional presence that could give his family confidence to grow securely.

Sam was sexually addicted, though as with any other type of addiction, he certainly wasn't willing or able to see his illness. His family history set him up to include sexual titillation as part of normal coping behavior for dealing with life's anxieties. It wasn't until he faced his wife's ultimatum that Sam began to look more seriously at himself. And Sam's first response to his wife's ultimatum? Anger and lashing out.

The Grieving Process (the exposure of a hidden sin)

Sam's experience gives me an opportunity to discuss the grieving process, especially in light of Sam's anger and lashing out in response to his wife's ultimatum. (The grieving process has a broad application, in this case to relational loss, rather than to the more familiar, narrow application to the death of a loved one.) An angry response on the part of the offending person is so common that it warrants some discussion.

Sam had been living in denial, the first stage of the grieving process. Denial doesn't mean that he didn't know what he was doing. But to rationalize his behavior, he had to minimize the seriousness of it. In other words, denial is simply the inability or unwillingness to see more fully what one is actually doing and the ramifications of such behavior.

It wasn't until Sam's wife confronted him with the seriousness of his offense that he began to see more clearly the consequences of his choices. Consistent with the grieving process, the second stage is often some form of anger. It is like an assault on our sensibilities. We feel exposed and vulnerable. We have lost our cover and can no longer hide. At this point our natural protective instincts kick in and we lash out in defense. Unfortunately, as in Sam's case, the damage at this stage is compounded because the action being exposed is really indefensible. At this point I try to warn men about their expression of anger during the grieving process, in hopes that they don't alienate their wives any more than they already have. Most often, however, by the time a couple comes for counseling, they have already experienced some of the defensive anger on the part of the offending spouse.

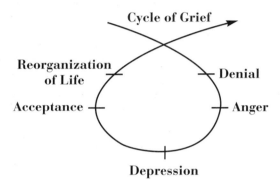

Once the denial and anger stages have been realized, it's usually time for a period of depression (loss of energy, profound sadness, helplessness) on the part of the offending spouse. This is a necessary part of the grieving process. However, it often seems to come at a time when more energy is required to deal with the hurt of the offended spouse. At this point the offended spouse will need to ask countless questions, often repeating the same questions over and over again. The offending spouse simply needs to endure this questioning for as long as it takes the offended spouse to move through her own grieving process (which includes anger as well).

When the major depression period begins to subside, the couple will eventually reach the stage of acceptance, though even this is only cognitive in nature. It's not until the final stage, what I call reorganization of life, that an emotional level of acceptance can be achieved. This is where the couple decides either to separate and divorce or to move forward together. Now the real work begins as the couple learns to craft a new relationship.

It is important to note that this grieving process is not as neat and simple as it first appears. Each person moves through the process at his own pace, and stages are frequently repeated and combined. But this model *does* seem to help people track their emotional responses as they go through the grieving process, giving them a greater measure of control in the midst of an experience that otherwise feels very out of control.

The damage done to Sam and Carol's relationship by Sam's sexual addiction was serious. With care and attention to one another and the grieving process, however, I am confident it can be overcome.

Eleven

The Words
"I Love You"

Michael, age 30

I didn't meet Michael until I had seen his wife, Therese, in counseling for several months. Therese came to me because of some recurring intimacy issues from childhood sexual abuse, and now she was beginning to have trouble with trust in her marriage. Consequently, even though our focus was initially on Therese, she eventually invited Michael to attend a session with her, and this began the process of working with them as a couple.

Certainly Therese had personal issues that she needed to address. However, it also became clear that Michael had been making some decisions that were detrimental to the marriage. Perhaps most notably, Michael had a difficult time allowing himself to get close to Therese emotionally. He often lied about trivial things. A significant percentage of his work involved travel (over which he had some control). But he had recently become a father, and was reevaluating his commitment as both a husband and parent.

Therese confronted Michael in counseling one day when she exposed the fact that he had been downloading Internet porn on his laptop computer. Due to her childhood experiences of betrayal by men, she was especially sensitive to this discovery. It also seemed to her that as a couple they were growing increasingly distant, and Michael was spending more time on the road. Michael obviously loved his son, but felt insecure about his abilities as a father.

As Michael and I sat in the room alone, I was very aware that he and I shared a culture that does not easily support the idea of two men allowing themselves to be vulnerable with each other. I needed to be careful not to move too close too fast, or I would risk losing the opportunity to work with Michael. Fortunately he was at a place in life where he desired to learn about marriage and family. And he was ready to talk about how his perspective on relationships was shaped by experiences in his family of origin.

Michael grew up in a middle-income family in which both parents worked outside the home. He felt very distinctly that he was on his own by the age of eleven. What he meant by this is that neither of his parents was readily available to him, physically or emotionally, from this point on. He even wondered why they bothered to have children (he had a younger brother) if they didn't want to spend time with them. If anyone was available, it was his father, though he tended to adopt a rather passive role in relation to Michael's mother, whom he described as domineering and emotionally distant.

Michael expressed a strong desire to make a positive contribution to his son's life, but he didn't know what to *do* with his son. We talked about how one of the most difficult things for us men to appreciate is the power of presence. Basically it has to do with the fact that just being present is *doing* something. Somehow our minds as men (I'm including myself here) have great trouble accepting that our time has any worth if we are not on the clock, accomplishing something, when, in fact, our very *presence* in the home is one of our most important callings. And underneath it all, we wonder (sometimes with help from our spouse) whether the quantity of our time with our children translates into significant quality of experience and benefit.

William Pollack, who is probably best known for his book *Real Boys,* helps us address the "quantity versus quality" question:

> . . . fathers in our study who were highly involved with their work, were satisfied with that work, and spent a fair amount of time at it could not spend equal amounts of time with their child. However, the quality of the time these "job-satisfied" fathers spent with their child directly and positively affected the child's mental health. Now, a word of caution is in order: I am not saying that fathers can abandon their families and the quality of connection will remain the same. What is clear from our study, however, is that work-invested fathers who care about their children and spend significant time with them—albeit not the same quantity of time as mothers do—can still have an important effect on the emotional well-being of their sons and daughters ("No Man Is an Island: Toward a New Psychoanalytic Psychology of Men," in *A New Psychology of Men,* edited by Ronald F. Levant and William S. Pollack, p. 52).

One of the most helpful images of a father's presence that I have come across is that of a tomato plant stake. A tomato plant has to have something to cling to as it grows upward. If it does not, the fruit will fall to the ground and rot. So the role of the father is to be a tomato plant stake. We place ourselves in the middle of the plant, and it begins to climb and grow and ripen. Not a very flattering image, but a necessary role.

As I listened to Michael, I felt the emotional flooding that comes with being vulnerable when a man has worked so hard to protect himself all of his life. Was it his flooding that I felt? Or was it my flooding? The answer to both questions was yes. And once again I was reminded that my work with men as a pastoral counselor is largely defined by my ability to help them learn a language by which to access difficult and confusing emotions. Michael wanted something better for his son. He wanted his son to enjoy true intimacy in relationships and a wide range of emotional expression.

I kept asking questions about Michael's relationship with his father, but each time he seemed more interested in addressing his challenges with his mother. (My personal issues tended to center more on my relationship with my father, but I needed to allow that another man may have a greater need to sort through his relationship with his mother.) In many ways she set the tone for the family, and Michael had never felt fully embraced by her. His expectations for marriage seemed to include the idea that women don't really want closeness in the end. I asked Michael to write a letter to his mother. And like my previous use of this letter-writing technique, I asked him to assume that his mother had died and requested the letter.

Mom —

I want to take this time and write a letter expressing how much you mean to me and how much I appreciate your love and support over the years. I know I have never really sat down and spoken with you about these things, probably because I felt embarrassed about speaking these words or maybe just because no one outside Therese has ever spoken these kinds of feelings to me. I know you love me even though you have really never said those words to me. To be quite honest, if you said "I love you," I'm not sure how I would react. I know you love me because of your actions and having been there for me when I needed you and Dad. Your actions mean more than words, but I think having both would have been terrific. I want to give Andrew and Therese both — words and acts of love. So I will start this letter with I Love You!

I know that I may have disappointed you in the past with the many wrongs that I did and because I never went into the career you wanted me to. I think you are proud of Darren and me, but it would be nice to have heard that once in awhile. The one thing that hurt me the most was that you would praise someone else but would never recognize my accomplishments. I don't know why it was easy for you to say something nice about someone else but not about your own sons or husband. Even until this day, you have never expressed your happiness with my family, my career, where we live, or my accomplishments in life. Criticism is fine, and I valued your opinions, but acknowledgment of both Darren's and my work would have meant so much to both of us.

You really have never let anything go if you perceived someone as hurting you. I think you and Dad need to have a talk and forgive each other for past issues that you both, but particularly you, carry with you. Your pent-up frustration and anger has been scary at times. I hope that you now have the peace to let go of the past that has angered you so.

I want you to know that I will do whatever is necessary to keep from falling into that trap. I still have my old habits of not wanting to talk and express my emotions, but with Therese's help, I will be able to work out problems instead of letting them fester over the years and degrade the quality of my life. You are such a great and caring person, I wish you could have been able to express yourself outwardly to me in my later years when I really could have used words of comfort. I also wish this for yourself, as you could have had a truly happy and content life in relation to your grandchildren and in all aspects of your life.

Michael began his letter with "Mom." Not "Dear Mom," just "Mom." And it wasn't until the end of the first paragraph that he says, "So I will start this letter with I Love You." In other words, tender emotions were felt but not easily spoken. In a very real way this was the first time Michael had ever uttered those words out loud in reference to his mother (he read the letter to me).

Life encompasses a few foundational beliefs that need not be filled with ambiguity or confusion. One such belief is a child's understanding that his parents love him and cherish him deeply. Michael had to assume too much. He had to work pretty hard at convincing himself that his mother loved him—he never heard the words "I Love You" (notice how he begins each of these three words with a capital letter). Now, in counseling, Michael is determined to both demonstrate and verbalize to his wife and son that he loves them. He doesn't want them to ever wonder about this truth.

Michael and I reflected on the ambiguities of life, the tension that all of us live with as we imagine how things should be and at the same time face how things actually are. Michael knows in his mind what he should be doing in his relationship with his wife and son, but he continues to do just the opposite. For example, he knows that he needs to ask for forgiveness and say "I love you," but instead he becomes defensive, withdraws, and throws himself into his work. We talked about St. Paul who, on close examination of himself, said: "What a wretched man I am! Who will rescue me from this body of death?" (Romans 7:24). Michael wants to be delivered. He wants to be set free to live a whole and God-pleasing life. We talked about faith as a process rather than a single event. And we asked for God's Spirit to indwell him so that he might be strengthened in his journey. Jesus was the only perfect man. Our perfection won't come until we reach the other side of heaven. Here we experience joy and sorrow, fear and comfort, life and death. But every child should know he is loved.

Michael reminded me of a child who is at the stage just before learning to think seriously about how his actions might affect others. He had learned at an early age to think primarily of himself because no one else would ever do so. He also learned at an early age that telling the truth was neither welcome nor safe because there was no hope for forgiveness—his mother's grudges were unbearable.

Michael had some emotional deficits in relation to intimacy, and this compounded Therese's personal struggles around some of the same issues. Both of them needed to learn that God had brought them together so that he could give them what they needed through each other, and that the harder they had to work at the marriage, the greater would be God's gifts to them. It was interesting to see that as Michael became healthier in his relationship with his wife, she too became healthier in relation to her history of child abuse. It is a good thing Therese came to me first, and became strong enough to confront Michael so that he could face himself. (Since beginning counseling, Michael has reduced his travel schedule by 50 percent and is amazed that he still has a job. Sometimes we have more options than we are willing to see.)

Twelve

Intimacy

Adam, age 34

Adam and his wife, Nancy, came to me after Nancy had been to individual counseling with another counselor and was then referred to me for marital counseling. The couple had been married three years and had a four-month-old baby. Adam had been married previously for three years. By the time Adam and Nancy came to me, Adam was leaning toward divorce.

I usually explain to married couples that I do three types of counseling. The first type is marriage counseling, in which both people are committed to making the marriage work. The second type is divorce counseling, in which at least one person has made up his or her mind that the marriage is not going to work. And the third type is what I call decision counseling. This is when at least one person isn't really sure which of the first two types of counseling to pick, and the most honest thing to say is that he or she is somewhere in the middle. At this point I ask which way the person is leaning. For Adam, he was leaning toward divorce. This provided a helpful benchmark for the work we were going to attempt together.

Adam described himself as a serious Christian. He and his wife had both recently come out of fundamentalism and into a more "grace-oriented" church tradition. They both expressed feeling oppressed in their former places of worship. Now they worshiped in a church where they received the twofold message that though they are sinners, they are not condemned: Christ paid the full price for their sins when he died on the cross. They eagerly expressed the faith that they could not merit their salvation and that Christ alone had satisfied God's demands on their behalf. There was just one problem: Adam was beginning to use his religious beliefs to avoid taking personal responsibility for his role in the breakdown of their marriage.

Adam had a history of short-lived relationships. His previous marriage had lasted only three years. And he had recently begun "helping" a single, female seminary student with a new ministry venture. "I have more in common with this woman than I do with my own wife. Besides, I'm not even sure my wife is a Christian. And I have begun to question her ability as a parent because she appears like a zombie when I come home from work. I think God wants a better environment for me and my daughter."

I challenged Adam to consider his emotional attachment to the seminary student. I asked him to devote himself to prayer and to ask God for guidance. Eventually, after a few sessions, I confronted Adam with his own belief system and told him that I believe God calls us to fully commit ourselves to our marriage whether we feel in love or not. In fact, the more difficult the marriage is may be an indication of how much God wants to teach us about ourselves and the meaning of true intimacy. Such a strong position would run the risk of alienating Adam from counseling, but if his belief system was genuine, he would have to wrestle with God over this one. No easy way out. Grace is never a license to disobey God.

The next week Adam called to say that his schedule would not allow him to make his regular appointment (more likely, we

had come too close to the heart of the matter in our previous session). The week after that, he called to reschedule for the same
reason. Finally, the third week, he came in to see me again. This
time he had a confession to make. He said that God had con-
victed him about his relationship with the seminary student and
that he had ended their relationship. He showed me a timeline he
had written outlining a series of romantic relationships in his life
that all ended with him leaving each person after having committed himself emotionally to another woman. "I'm afraid that
my current situation is simply a repeat of this old familiar pattern. I need God to help me stop this cycle. And I think it's possible for me to trace this failure of intimacy back to my
relationship with my mother." I asked him to write a letter.

Dear Mom,

As I have begun to focus on the relationship that you and I have
shared, several pervasive feelings have dominated my analysis. You have
set a standard that on the one hand I seem to have met, but any future
activity must be compared to this standard, and disaster will impend on
me in a vicious downward spiral if I do not maintain this standard.

I love you but know that I cannot depend on you at all in times of
trouble, despair, and need. Even when you give advice to Joyce [Adam's
sister] or to me, you become upset when we challenge you with it or suggest how you could handle things better. Your priority is always your
own emotional satisfaction, even when those that you love are suffering.

But our relationship has always been about you anyway, hasn't it.
You need me emotionally, and I can support you. I am thankful for that.
That attribute of our relationship is what provides foundation for us. We
should be thankful for your emotional need and my ability to help you.
And why would our relationship now be any different than it has always
been? From the time we moved to Baltimore, when I was in the first
grade, your attention has never been focused on me. Grandma and your
business were your priorities. During junior high and high school, Dad

was my only parent. You only became involved when I was in trouble. And then your focus was on how I had embarrassed you. Once again, I was just an inconvenience. You say, "But I worked so you could have things." But any gift that you gave was really an attempted purchase of my love, with a summary rendition of how that caused you to sacrifice in some way and a reminder that you had done something else for me. Things were not important to me, and I had plenty of my own money to buy them anyway. You say, "We used to go out to eat together when Dad was out of town." That is true. I was your companion, and I enjoyed it very much. But the focus was always on you and making you feel better, which was fine with me because I never knew any different.

I love you very much, and it certainly helps me to deal with these things. I feel sorry for you. I wish that you were free to truly love.

Adam

The letter feels forced, as though Adam is attempting to write with a style and vocabulary beyond his ability. And yet this is characteristic of Adam. He expends a great deal of energy trying to present himself as above everything and everyone else. He is the untouchable one. Perhaps this has something to do with the standard that he writes about. Unfortunately, others often experience his personal strivings as controlling. I'm guessing this is similar to the way in which he experiences his mother.

As I listened to Adam read his letter, I felt a strange gnawing in my stomach. It sounded as though Adam was using his letter to absolve himself of all responsibility by placing the blame on his mother. Suddenly I realized that my issues with my own mother were blurring my view. If Adam had been writing to his father, I wouldn't have had the same internal response. "Let him unload," I would've said to myself. But this was different. This was his mother. And I had a difficult time admitting just how deeply I was affected by the way that I needed my mother's nurture and protection.

Adam was actually being vulnerable as he reflected on how his mother recruited him at an early age to meet the emotional needs that should have been met by his father. He remembers feeling both flattered and overwhelmed by her expectations. Unfortunately, he and his sister, Joyce, never felt that they quite measured up to their mother's expectations. "My sister lives near my parents, but rarely goes to see them. My way of dealing with my mother was to move across the country, away from her." However, geographic distance doesn't seem to make much of a difference. Once a parental relationship is established, it stays with us like an imprint. It's eventually better to face it than to run, especially because our own children have a way of reflecting our personal struggles in their lives.

I have learned to pay particularly close attention to the way letters begin and end. Often these seemingly simple greetings are loaded with more substance than might be expected from an otherwise stylized address. In Adam's case, he summarized the heart of the issue with his mother in the words, "I wish that you were free to truly love." This is Adam's personal struggle. He has never allowed himself to get close to someone and remain close. Up until the crisis of his current marriage, he used whatever means available to create distance between himself and others. Oh, he was charming, but never genuinely close.

When Adam first came for counseling, he would frequently use investment language to describe his relationship with his wife. "I feel as though I have made a considerable investment without gaining much of a return. What I need to do is simply cut my losses and move on." He also used religion, questioning whether his wife was truly a Christian believer and therefore committed to the marriage. "Maybe it wasn't God's will that we marry after all," he had suggested more than once. Either way, he was looking for a justifiable "out." In fact, if it hadn't been for the fact that he and Nancy had a child, I don't know if Adam would have ever been willing to take a second look at himself. The whole process was so shaky, from my perspective, that I was prepared for Adam to go either way in the relationship. But a baby has a way of sneaking past our defenses like a Trojan horse. (Isn't it amazing—and so *perfect*—that God chose to come to us as a baby?)

Adam's current marriage has deeply challenged his old pattern of cutting himself off emotionally from those who get too close. He demonstrates the power of old habits and the ability to rationalize, even from a faith perspective. But his conscience has been taken captive by the word of God, in which he hears a strong message about the sanctity of marriage. And as he looks his newborn child in the face, he wonders what she will see as she looks back at him.

Adam asks God to help him disengage from a recent emotional attachment to another woman. It was difficult, but he expresses feeling freedom from having said good-bye to the other woman. He can now begin to focus more intently on his immediate family. And he is learning to ask God the question, "What do you intend to teach me through this marriage?"

The Loop of Intimacy

Adam's story lends itself to a discussion of what I call the loop of intimacy. This loop is a model that helps men and women identify where they are in relation to the experience of closeness and distance in their relationships. This loop also helps each person identify with which of these two, closeness and distance, they may have the greatest difficulty. From a gender standpoint, for example, I often find that women have more difficulty with the experience of distance, while men will frequently have more difficulty with the experience of closeness. (This is a generalization, however, and should not be pushed too far.) The loop of intimacy looks like this:

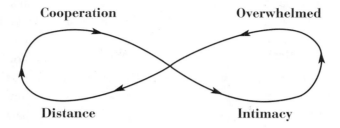

Cooperation **Overwhelmed**

Distance **Intimacy**

A couple begins at the first emotional stage, cooperation, before moving on to intimacy. Cooperation could be any activity that is done together, like planning a trip or planting a garden. It doesn't really matter what the activity is, as long as it includes mutually supportive time together. In other words, the couple isn't just watching a video or spending "parallel" time together. (Parallel time is when a couple may be in the same house, even the same room, but each one is devoted to separate interests.) They need to have sustained, ongoing interaction.

Once a couple has been together at the stage of cooperation in a mutually supportive way, they eventually move toward the stage of intimacy. Intimacy, as used here, is not to be equated with sex. Sex can certainly be a part of intimacy, but intimacy is a much larger, foundational part of the relationship. In other words, true intimacy occurs first and foremost outside of the bedroom.

The best definition that I have found for intimacy is "the ability to share pain." Pain refers to the sharing of vulnerabilities, fears, dashed hopes, faded dreams, and disappointments in self and others. This is the glue that holds a marriage together. As a couple feels at ease together and trusts that the other is listening to understand, not to fix or criticize, then each person begins to share more personal pain. This is done in an atmosphere of trust so that no one fears that the information will be thrown back in her or his face at a later date.

Intimacy as defined here is an intensive experience. You know when you have achieved this stage. You feel a connectedness that begins to explain what the scriptures mean when they say that a husband and wife become one flesh. Like peeling an onion or layers of clothing, each time a couple moves around the loop, they expose a little more. Again, sex may occur at this stage, but not necessarily. (However, even in a marriage in which one partner, particularly the woman, claims she does not feel ready for sex, it is probably because the couple has not recently spent enough time at the cooperation stage.)

No one can stand to remain at any one emotional stage on the loop indefinitely. There has to be movement (note the directional arrows on the loop). This means that intimacy eventually gives way to the stage that I call overwhelmed. You might find a better word to use here, but the main idea is that the intensity of closeness becomes smothering, even oppressive. Some movement toward the emotional stage called distance is necessary to allow each person the opportunity to take a deep breath and experience the feeling of being a separate individual.

The stage of distance is not a "stepping away from" the relationship. No one steps out of the loop. There simply seems to be a need for some self-reflective time (reading a book, riding a bike, taking a walk) before re-engaging more fully at the stage of cooperation and thus beginning the loop all over again.

Distance will be achieved consciously or subconsciously. If achieved subconsciously, distance will likely occur with a flare-up between a couple at a time when everything seemed to be going well. However, a couple can learn to make this movement more conscious by recognizing that the subtle irritations that eventually accompany intense closeness are a signal that the couple is beginning to feel overwhelmed and needs some distance or time alone.

Some people (most often women) feel threatened by the experience of the distance stage because they are afraid it means the end of closeness or intimacy. It is helpful, then, to remember that the loop is continuous, and that all emotional stages are necessary.

Others (most often men) feel threatened by the experience of intimacy. This is, in part, because they haven't learned a language for emotions, and also because they tend to operate with a narrow definition of the concept of intimacy, one that restricts its use to the bedroom. For example, a number of women have told me that they never hear the words "I love you" except during lovemaking.

We may apply this loop of intimacy to Adam's case. Remember that his mother had taught Adam, at an early age, that women needed him to be available emotionally, but that he wasn't supposed to need anyone himself. In other words, Adam learned that closeness, or intimacy, was threatening because it demanded a one-sided response.

As Adam grew older, he would get caught in an intensely close relationship with a woman and then actually step out of the loop as a way to gain some much needed distance. Adam saw intimacy as an all-or-nothing experience, and his responses were sabotaging his relationships. The only way he could balance out closeness and distance was to begin a new relationship while still in an old relationship. Thankfully for him, for Nancy, and for their daughter, he began to see this pattern and was willing to ask for help.

Thirteen

Polarity Management

Allen, age 45

Allen and his wife, Peggy, came to see me after several years of feeling as though they had been, as they put it, "drifting apart." They loved each other and had three wonderful children together, but they just didn't seem to connect anymore in vital ways. Both were relatively happy in their careers and shared many of the same basic commitments to family and church. But the spark had faded. The old enthusiasm about being with each other had disappeared. They had been stuck in a rut for a long time and didn't see any way out. What brought them in for counseling was their observation of other couples at church who demonstrated a closeness in their relationships that they knew was missing from their own.

Allen and Peggy brought many strengths to their relationship. Both came from intact families with a strong sense of tradition and stability. Allen was a high school principal, and Peggy was a computer analyst. As a couple they shared the same financial goals for retirement as well as for their children's higher education, and planned accordingly. In many ways this was one of the healthiest couples I had ever seen in counseling, and I told them so. Together we decided that they would most benefit from an educational approach that sought to enrich their marriage. They didn't need traditional therapy, but neither did they want to continue with the status quo. Something needed to change.

The enrichment approach that I adopted for Allen and Peggy presupposed a pretty high degree of individual and marital health. Enrichment is always a goal with couples. However, more emphasis frequently needs to be placed on the therapeutic side until couples develop a strong enough foundation on which to build. Unfortunately, I find too many couples are referred to enrichment seminars when what they really need is therapy. This often results in a couple feeling worse than they did before the seminar. Allen and Peggy, on the other hand, were a resourceful couple who just needed to get back on track toward a more fulfilling marriage.

I have decided to include this couple in the book because their story allows me to reflect on the importance of making a distinction between problems-to-be-solved and polarities-to-be-managed. Frequently I see couples whose difficulties have come about because they are approaching polarities as though they were problems-to-be-solved. Such was the case with Allen and Peggy. I'll explain first what I mean by these two concepts, problems and polarities, and then apply them to our couple.

A problem-to-be-solved is an either/or proposition. You have two distinct, mutually exclusive choices. For example, a couple chooses to provide for their children's higher education or they don't so choose. They cannot do both at the same time. Allen and Peggy were usually on the same page with this type of issue. If a major budgeting problem came up, they could work through it together and solve it.

Where Allen and Peggy had trouble was in dealing with what I call polarities-to-be-managed. A polarity is made up of two opposite actions that require each other for both to exist. My favorite example is the act of breathing itself. You have two opposite actions, inhaling and exhaling. You can't have one without the other. It might feel really good to inhale until you reach a certain point and need to exhale, which itself feels really good until you reach a certain point and need to inhale again, which itself feels really good until . . . ; you get the idea.

Breathing is not a problem-to-be-solved. No one would argue that inhaling is a problem that should be solved by exhaling, any more than a person would argue that exhaling is a problem that needs to be solved by inhaling. Both are required. It's a both/and proposition. If either pole is missing, be it inhaling or exhaling, you have neither one. It's called death. (Other examples of polarities would be work/rest, individual/group, leader/follower, rules/relationships, and so on.)

Couples often make the mistake of approaching polarities-to-be-managed as though they were problems-to-be-solved. Allen and Peggy struggled with what I call the rules/relationships polarity. Peggy preferred to focus on the rules side while Allen preferred to focus on the relationships side. Notice the use of the word "preferred." This is important because each person tended to have a more dominant preference toward one side (pole) or the other. (Fortunately, breathing is an involuntary action, so we don't have this problem.)

Allen's focus on relationships was a real strength. He was able to adjust easily to the needs of different people, whether it was his teaching staff at school, his wife, or his three children. However, he also had a tendency to say yes too quickly to others' requests and *then* look for a way to actually follow through with his commitment. This often left him feeling overwhelmed and frustrated by the demands on his time and energy. Peggy, on the other hand, was stronger in the rules department, and as such emphasized the importance of consistency and fairness in dealing with people. She also had a natural tendency to say no about a new idea, and then warm up to it after giving it further thought. This sometimes made her appear unfeeling and inflexible toward the people in her life, including Allen.

Over time Allen and Peggy had developed some pretty hardened views toward each other's individual styles or preferences in this rules/relationships polarity. Allen perceived his relationships approach as right and Peggy's rules approach as wrong, while Peggy saw it as just the opposite. Instead of seeing a polarity that requires both poles for each to exist, they saw this polarity as a problem-to-be-solved. "He's too wishy-washy," said Peggy of Allen. "She's too inflexible," said Allen of Peggy. It was as if Peggy was suggesting that inhaling (or relationships) is a problem and exhaling (rules) is the solution. Allen would simply reverse this statement.

This couple needed to learn that each of them had a preference for a different side of the same polarity, and that the answer was for each to embrace the other as having a necessary strength. Together this couple could become more complementary and mutually supportive, and thereby discover that each was a gift from God to help balance out the other. At any given time, the need may exist for more of an emphasis on one pole or the other, like inhaling or exhaling, but both are required for each to exist. Without a sense of rules there wouldn't be any consistency in life, and without a sense of relationships this world would be a very cold place to live.

Another factor that played into the rules/relationships polarity for Allen and Peggy related to their respective cultures of origin. Allen was Hispanic, and Peggy was Germanic. Allen's family background encouraged more fluid and flexible relationships with extended family. It was not uncommon for Allen to invite extended family in transition to live with his family. He felt it was a privilege and an honor to be able to help in this way. Peggy, on the other hand, whose background encouraged greater independence and a strong sense of boundary formation, was not very comfortable with opening her home so easily. She constantly felt compelled to protect her time and space with Allen and her children. The presence of extended family members felt intrusive and disrespectful.

I developed an immediate affinity with Peggy around the issue of inviting extended family to live in the same house. However, my culture of origin is also Germanic, and so I needed to listen carefully to Allen to appreciate his cultural perspective. Flexible and fluid living arrangements were central to his identity. Family members took care of one another no matter what the situation.

I was strangely drawn to Allen's cultural distinction as somehow providing a necessary corrective for what has become such an individualistic ideal in our society. In many ways I believe we're out of balance in our attempts to demonstrate our independence. We inhale too much and need to learn how to exhale more.

While I found a way to embrace Allen's cultural background as a definite strength for his marriage, I also had the distinct impression that Allen sometimes felt he had to choose between honoring his wife and honoring his father. He spoke of his father with great pride and fondness. An immigrant from Mexico, Allen's father labored on U.S. border farms most of his life, until he died of cancer that had gone untreated because of a lack of medical insurance. Allen struggled with guilt over the fact that he had attained so much more educationally and financially than his father. And his attempts to provide a home for other family members who were in transition almost seemed to be driven by a fear of dishonoring his father. What Allen needed to decide, though, was how to best serve the needs of his wife and children—a difficult struggle at best.

Another polarity that Allen and Peggy struggled with (or more importantly, had stopped struggling with) is what I call the external/internal polarity. Some people use the words extrovert/introvert, but I find that these words are frequently misunderstood and so prefer the words external/internal.

Allen was more external and Peggy was more internal. I say "more" because as with all polarities, we each have both poles operating. We just tend to prefer one pole and underutilize the other. The trick is to learn one's preference and how to maintain personal balance in relation to others. In this case Allen and Peggy needed to find a way to balance the external/internal polarity in their marriage.

An external person can easily be misunderstood by internal folks as someone who always has something to say about everything and speaks before thinking. But this is not fair or an accurate assessment of an external person. Rather, a strong external person "speaks to think." He or she thinks out loud. He puts his ideas out in front of him verbally (externally), and then receives feedback and corrects or moves forward in his thinking. What can lead to misunderstanding is the fact that an external person also tends to speak with a certain strength or conviction. If you didn't know that he was just thinking out loud, you might conclude that he has made up his mind. Case closed. No more discussion. However, this generally isn't true at all. The external person just needs to get it out there.

An internal person also can be easily misunderstood. Imagine a work group gathered around a table to collaborate on a project. Invariably someone (an external person) will suggest brainstorming ideas. As you look around the table, you will notice several people readily throwing out their ideas. At the same time, you will probably see a couple of people who remain rather quiet and reserved. These are the more internal people in the group. Unfortunately, the external folks might draw the conclusion that these quieter people are not truly committed to the project; if they were, they would be forthcoming with their ideas, like the external folks. In reality, these people are probably doing some important thinking about the subjects at hand, but are doing so internally. What they seem to need is for someone to ask for their opinion. They need to know that it's their turn to speak, at which point the group will discover that some wonderful processing has been going on.

Allen and Peggy sometimes ran into this trouble. It would seem to Peggy that Allen dominated the conversation by sharing everything on his mind. Allen would become frustrated with Peggy for not readily sharing her thoughts. Peggy would frequently conclude, prematurely, that Allen had made up his mind. In this instance it helped this couple to see that each was operating with a preferred style on a shared polarity. Allen could learn to stop talking and ask for Peggy's opinion, and Peggy could request that Allen tell her when he feels that he has made up his mind about something.

Other distinguishing traits of the external/internal polarity are manifested in the way each person experiences social settings and time alone, and in the way each person experiences the increase or depletion of energy in relation to self and others. For example, the external person enjoys talking with many people in a group setting and is energized by the experience. The internal person, on the other hand, can interact in groups but tends to focus the interaction on just one or two people. Instead of being energized by the interaction, the internal person experiences an energy depletion. To get his personal bucket of energy replenished, he will need to spend some time alone (taking a walk or reading a book, for example).

Allen was a strong external, and Peggy was a strong internal. Each one's personality fit well with their respective careers. Neither one, however, spent her or his entire workday engaged only in the preferred style. This could result in some real misunderstandings on the home front. For example, on days when Allen's work required him to sit behind a computer instead of interact with people, he came home with a need to be with others to restore his personal energy level. But on days when Peggy's work required more interaction with people, she came home with the need to spend time alone to restore her personal energy level.

Over the years Allen and Peggy had developed some uncharitable views toward each other. Peggy thought that Allen was overly focused on others and underfocused on her and the immediate family, while Allen thought that Peggy was frequently aloof and unresponsive to his need for time with others. Instead of appreciating that the other had a stronger preference for one pole or the other on a shared polarity, they had concluded that one way of being was right and the other was wrong. In this instance some practical considerations were helpful. Allen could give Peggy some time alone after work before expecting her to more fully engage with the family. For her part, Peggy could plan some social events with Allen and thereby feel more prepared for such activity in advance.

All of us have many polarities to navigate and negotiate every day, from the work/rest polarity to the individual/group polarity. Each one of us tends to have a particular preference for one pole or the other. The important thing is to recognize that polarities are not problems-to-be-solved. It's not a matter of suggesting that one pole is right and the other is wrong. The key lies in recognizing when one pole or the other needs attention. In this way couples who have different preferences can learn from each other and see the other as bringing some necessary balance to their life as a couple.

In the church, I often find that people have an opportunity to feel the "wholeness" of polarities when they embrace the individual/group polarity inherent in St. Paul's analogy of the church as the body of Christ. "There are many parts," the individual pole, Paul wrote, "but one body," which is the group pole (1 Corinthians 12:20). Uniqueness, individual expression, different functions, services, and gifts, but a shared mission and vision: "one Lord, one faith, one baptism; one God and Father of all" (Ephesians 4:5-6). Perhaps this concept of polarities can help us achieve greater spiritual depth in our relationships, especially our most important relationships: our marriages and families.

I remember distinctly an observation that Allen made about the differences in the cultures of Mexico and the United States. He said that he has always struggled with the question of what he does for a living when meeting someone for the first time in the United States. They ask, "What do you do?" In Mexico, though, says Allen, people ask; "Who is your father?" "What is your family name?" This observation reflects another polarity, that of being and doing. It also has significant implications for Christians. How freeing and healthy it would be for people in the church to pay more attention to their identity, or *being*, as people of God than to what they as individuals do in the world for money and status. Allen's observation can also help us see that God, our heavenly father, demonstrates—by both being and doing—his conviction that he loves each and every one of us for who we are.

Conclusion

My desire throughout this book has been to both encourage and challenge the reader to extend the voice of God, who spoke from heaven toward his son, Jesus, saying, "Behold, my son, whom I love." God's love for his son was so great that he wanted everyone to know it. What pride God demonstrated. What joy and pleasure he expressed. Oh, that we might take our cue from God and begin to cherish and behold our own dear children more fully. The outcome, the benefits, the payoff, the rewards—call it what you want—can be great beyond measure.

In many ways this book is intended to be more of an experience than a formal treatise on the male psyche. And it should be obvious that I have placed myself alongside the boys and men in their journeys rather than above or detached from them. It takes a lot more effort to work with people this way, but I also find it to be far more effective. Jesus, for example, didn't remain on shore as his disciples tossed in the wind and waves. He got into the boat with them. My job is to get into the boat with others and provide a reassuring, calm presence in the midst of the wind, waves, and storms.

I want to conclude with one last case study. The man in this story is older than those we heard from earlier. Robert is fifty-nine and represents some of the older men who are seeking counseling in increasing numbers. These men have gone the way of the boys and younger men previously discussed, but now their own children are nearly grown and they are looking back at their lives with considerable grief and regret. They wonder if it is too late to become a vital part of their children's lives. For me this is an important opportunity to come full circle in my relationship with my own father, as I learn to bring a message of hope and forgiveness to these men.

Robert, age 59

Robert and Cindy came to counseling with the request that I help them with the issue of their twenty-three-year-old son, Nick, who was still living at home. "He takes advantage of us, and doesn't seem remotely interested in moving forward with his life," said Cindy. "If you ask me, he's just plain lazy," chimed Robert. I rarely see a situation in which responsibility is placed so fully on the child, even an adult child. After all, the parents were *allowing* the son to live there. My curiosity was piqued.

Even though this couple said they wanted Nick to be on his own, they had compelling reasons for maintaining the status quo. Robert had traveled in his work for many years, usually spending four or five days away from home each week. He was a weekend husband and father. Cindy had learned to cope with Robert's absence by defining herself almost exclusively as a mother. They had three children, with Nick being the middle child. The oldest had gone to college, graduated, and lived and worked elsewhere in the state. The youngest was about to graduate from high school and was planning to attend college. Cindy was facing the loss of all of her children, which would leave her at home by herself. She believed Nick needed to move on, perhaps even with a push, but she had also counted on his presence to help fill the void of Robert's absence. And Robert counted on Nick to meet the needs that he was unavailable to meet. This couple was facing a major life transition.

We could have spent a lot of time talking about how things got to this point in the family. Although we did need to look at their history, the more pressing issue was what would happen to the marriage if the adult son actually moved out. I suggested that the couple implement a plan for the son's move-out date and that Robert find work that required less travel. This opened the door to the critical issues facing Robert and Cindy. "I don't really feel needed at home," Robert said. "I'm not sure Robert and I would know how to get along together if he was home all the time," responded Cindy. Now we were getting somewhere.

Nick definitely needed a push. He was not motivated to change his situation. He had a good thing going. When I visited with him alone, we discussed his work hours and budget. He was supposed to work full-time, but frequently missed hours and days because, as he said, "I just didn't feel like going in." He also couldn't account for three- to five-hundred dollars a month, which he said went toward the purchase of "stuff." This guy was having a good time. His housing and food were taken care of, leaving him with all the spending money he could want. What would he gain by moving out on his own? And besides, his mother needed him to do some of the chores around the house. "I earn my keep," he claimed.

Robert and Cindy devised a six-month plan for Nick to move out on his own. Within two weeks of presenting these new expectations, Nick informed them that he had found a roommate with whom to share an apartment, and by the end of the six months, he had moved out. He came over for dinner a couple times a week, but he was beginning to experience a more responsible lifestyle. (I usually find young people to be amazingly resourceful when necessary.)

Cindy seemed especially pleased that she and Robert had made the decision about their son and implemented it together. For the first time in a long time, this couple felt they were on the same page. Now they needed to more fully face their marriage, which meant that Robert would have to answer the question, "Does she need me beyond providing a paycheck?" As Robert and I talked about his transition away from work and back toward home, he began to exhibit symptoms commonly associated with depression. It turned out that in seeing Robert once a week, I had only seen him on his "up" day. I discovered that this man suffered from a low-grade depression throughout the week, while he was on the road, and that due to impotence, he and his wife had not had sexual relations for several months. Not only did he not feel needed at home, he didn't even feel like a fully functioning man. The only place he felt he could demonstrate some competence was on the job.

Robert was an intelligent man with a sarcastic, sometimes biting, wit. He also demonstrated tenderness toward his family, although Cindy commented once that the only time he expressed such tender feelings was in counseling. Robert responded, "That's what we're here for, to talk about all of this stuff." During this one hour each week, Robert had permission to say what was in his heart. And my presence as a younger man somehow seemed to facilitate his openness.

As I listened to Robert and observed his awkwardness with his family, I felt a deep sense of compassion for him. He had taken a wrong turn years ago when he decided to work (and live) away from his wife and children more than half of the time. He had missed so many important events, like his son's sixth birthday party and his daughter's junior high band concert. In fact, according to his family, he was *never* present to celebrate achievements. Now he wanted a relationship with each family member, and didn't know how to tell them. He wondered if it was too late. I assured him that I rarely found it to be too late. (In this I discovered a sympathetic voice for my own father.)

Robert would have to face the fact that he could never recover what had been lost in the past. It was too late to attend his son's birthday party or go to his daughter's band concert, but the question now was what to do in those relationships from this point forward. He would probably always grieve the loss of that earlier relationship formation, and his kids will always look back and wonder what could have been. But if he was willing to humble himself now, he could still build something great.

Robert was beginning to make a significant middle-life correction: the male shift from doing to being, from activities to relationships. But as he began to focus more on relationships, he came face-to-face with the losses that had resulted from his earlier work and travel choices—and he was depressed. He wondered, seriously, whether it was too late to be a husband and father.

With retirement just around the corner, Robert had only some stock options to show for all of his time and effort. He wondered what experiences from their relationship with him would sustain his children for the long haul. How would his absence shape their own expectations for marriage and family? At this point, who cares about stock options?

I see Robert's eyes begin to tear as we talk about his hopes and dreams for the future. I want him to know the depth of God's love and mercy for him as God's own dear child. I observe elements of my own father in Robert, and I begin to see my father differently—as more vulnerable—as God's dear son in need of mercy and grace. Robert has been a gift to me from God. Now I just hope Robert can see himself as a gift from God to his wife and children. He is more than his sin. He is a forgiven child of God.

OTHER RESOURCES FROM AUGSBURG

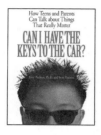

Can I Have the Keys to the Car? by Terry and Sean Paulson
128 pages, 0-8066-3836-2

This father and son team have written a reassuring and practical book that helps teens and parents talk together, search together, and laugh together about life's tough issues. They use humor, stories, and quotes from the Bible to explore the relevance of faith for the tough decisions teens have to make.

The Gift to Listen, the Courage to Hear by Cari Jackson
128 pages, 0-8066-4552-0
The Gift to Listen, the Courage to Hear interweaves listening techniques with spiritual principles that emphasize the importance of listening and provide a framework for more effective listening.

Finding Your Way by Scott Montgomery
192 pages, 0-8066-3870-2

Our personalities have potential for spiritual and emotional growth by using the self-compass with its four points of love, assertion, weakness, and strength. The reader learns how to navigate through the internal and external conflicts, pressures, and barriers that work against personal growth and wholeness.

A Forgiving Heart edited by Lyn Klug
176 pages, 0-8066-3997-0

A Forgiving Heart lets readers know they are not alone. This collection of powerful prayers offers understanding and new perspectives, providing healing for our relationship with God, ourselves, family and friends, in our communities, and among nations.

Available wherever books are sold.